Who Named the Knife

A BOOK OF MURDER AND MEMORY

Who Named the Knife

a book of murder and memory

LINDA SPALDING

McCLELLAND & STEWART

Hardcover edition published 2006
Trade paperback edition published 2007

Library and Archives Canada Cataloguing in Publication

Spalding, Linda
    Who named the knife / Linda Spalding.

ISBN: 978-0-7710-8224-5 (bound)
ISBN: 978-0-7710-8231-3 (pbk.)

    1. Acker, Maryann. 2. Spalding, Linda. 3. Murder–Hawaii.
4. Murderers–Hawaii–Biography. 5. Authors, Canadian (English)–20th
century–Biography. I. Title. II. Title: Who named the knife: A book of
murder and memory.

HV6533.H39S62 2005   364.152'3'09969   C2005-903392-4

We acknowledge the financial support of the Government of Canada
through the Book Publishing Industry Development Program and that of
the Government of Ontario through the Ontario Media Development
Corporation's Ontario Book Initiative. We further acknowledge the support
of the Canada Council for the Arts and the Ontario Arts Council for our
publishing program.

Typeset in Adobe Garamond by M&S, Toronto
Printed and bound in Canada

This book is printed on acid-free paper that is 100% recycled, ancient-forest
friendly (100% post-consumer recycled).

McClelland & Stewart Ltd.
75 Sherbourne Street
Toronto, Ontario
M5A 2P9
www.mcclelland.com

1 2 3 4 5   11 10 09 08 07

For Michael

"Justice had been done, and I belonged to the nation of criminals . . ."

– Peter Handke, Across (1986)

The first time I visited Hawaii it was still a territory, not yet the fiftieth American state, and to my vivid fourteen-year-old Kansas imagination, it was another world. I was visiting my brother and his wife in the summer of 1958. He'd been born ten years before me and by the time I could measure anything, he'd left home. He would not be a lawyer like our father. He would not wear a suit or drink highballs or join the navy. He saw that I was unhappy (we both knew the brooding temper in the Kansas house) and he took me out to Hanauma Bay, where he taught me courage by telling me to relax, to breathe, to go with the waves. Once, we were swimming over the coral looking down through our masks when I saw something in a crevasse where the water was not even very deep. It was a moray eel with a cold, blank look over an open throat and murderous teeth.

When I married, I moved with my husband to Hawaii. To the way, as my mother put it, I thought life should be. Of course it was changed. The landscape was different. There was no room for taro, the mainstay of the Hawaiian diet, or for the stone heiau *dedicated to Hawaiian gods. The past had disappeared, as it always does, but there were temple stones scattered in the grass. I tried to belong.*

I

When my husband and I divorced, I stayed in Hawaii and raised our two girls. Then there was a murder and a trial. The yellow notebook I kept.

Years later, to find that yellow book containing my notes, the mistake I had made. I had changed countries, changed lives. And I had left the past unfinished.

HONOLULU

I

Murder. In such a place.

From above, from the highway, it looks like a planet must have fallen into it, the round bowl edges of this bay are so perfect. Below the surface of the water, amazing fish can be seen living their lives in the coral. This is a place where children play in the waves, where parents sit on the sand, where people float, looking down. A swimmer can pause, roll over, blink a few times, and look up at the hills that surround this blue water. The hills feel protective, a barrier between the world of invention and this place.

So it must have looked to Larry Hasker in the last minutes of his life. He had been casual with his captors. "So this is a robbery? I can't believe it." He got out of the car with his shirt unbuttoned, his rubber slippers moving over the rocks. Up at the cusp, above the parking lot, the terrain is rough. Even through the slippers, he must have felt the jolts of stone and brush and dirt. He had smoked a joint in the car. He was young, twenty years old, and almost relaxed. On a ridge within sight of the highway, he turned and looked down. It was past midnight in the month of June, 1978. The moon was high. It threw its reflected light on the ocean so that the water looked like metal heated over flame. Molten. He breathed in and reached down for himself, opened his fly. Looking at water and night. The stars were there too. And his captors.

There is no shame in dying with a shirt open or pants, dying in the act of emptying oneself. In such a place.

The girl who discovered the body was taking a walk before work, noticing the dusty smell of kiawe above the bay, the pungent smell of seaweed, the smell of a place where ocean and land meet. It was early in the morning, but when she saw a slipper lying in the brush, she was not surprised. Near any beach, such a forgotten slipper is not unusual, although this one wasn't broken; its thong was intact. She saw the slipper and then she saw a human foot covered in flies. It was a Monday morning and nobody was there to hear, but she screamed.

So it begins with a body on the side of the road that leads from Hanauma Bay to the Kalanianaole Highway on the windward side of O'ahu – this story of murder, on the island where I lived. The body was lying twenty-five feet from that highway among rocks, thorns, and brush. The shirt was untorn. There were no scratches, no bruises, no cuts on the flesh. There were just two wounds: one on the right side of his head and one on the outside surface of a leg.

What happens in such a place, on such a beach, is quickly forgotten in any season. What happens can so easily wash away. Even above the tide line, far above it, a third bullet can get lodged in the sand, can be plucked at by birds, can be sent down the slope by a vagrant wind. A body can be ignored until it is past recognition, until its bones and teeth must be studied; it can be eaten; it can merge with the elements; it can be nosed at by wandering dogs. But this is a beach for children and families, a place to be walked along and sat upon. And what is there left of Larry Hasker here? Blood. Piss. A fragment of rubber slipper. He'd stood in the brush above the sea with its luminous sheen. One of his slippers had fallen off. He'd turned, unzipped and zipped. Then he'd been shot.

Once in an ankle. Once in the head.

Someone, it must have been, with lousy aim.

2

In 1978 I was a white, Midwestern American living on the windward side of O'ahu with my two daughters. I was a single mother then, running a child-care agency for low-income families, and I must have read about the murder of Larry Hasker in the morning paper. Another syndicate killing, I must have thought.

In those days, the morning paper was stuffed in my mailbox before I got up. I had to walk across the front yard in whatever I had worn to bed and step on the sleeping grass, which stung my feet. I'd have made myself a pot of coffee and given myself until ten o'clock to get to work because it was summer and I was my own boss. I'd have sat outside under the tin roof of the first house I'd ever owned – a house hard won and loved by me as no other. I'd have sat on one of the two basket chairs and read about the murder and I'd have thought about my father because it was a reflex. He had been dead for six years at the time of the murder, but I'd have thought about him and about my brother, who had taken me out to Hanauma Bay. Neither of us had ever seen our father in court, but all my life I had imagined him there.

3

Four years later, when I was summoned for jury duty, I had forgotten about the body lying under kiawe trees in the thorny brush above Hanauma Bay. It was 1982 and I was one of a pool of people who would be questioned by lawyers – both prosecution and defence – for any one of several trials. I was working for public television by then, across the mountains in Honolulu, and I was glad to be called. It would mean double pay for one thing, but there were other reasons that were more personal. I was about to move to Canada with my daughters. I had met someone and I was ready to give up the house, the job, the dog, everything. But this would be a last chance to leave a little mark of myself on the island where I had lived for fourteen years. And it was a chance to test myself on my father's ground.

For two days, I sat with seventy potential jurors, all of us being questioned about our backgrounds and habits and beliefs in a process known as voir dire, which means to tell the truth. Lawyers on both sides tried to weed out jurors who were likely to vote against them. Each of us was carefully studied.

During those two days, I was challenged by the prosecutors of two separate trials and sent back to the jury pool. An elderly friend said that in his opinion smart people didn't belong on juries. And a middle-aged man in the jury pool seemed to agree. He told me that what the court wanted were uneducated people, "the ones who maybe don't have the knowledge of right and wrong."

On the third day the remnants of the pool – those who had not yet been selected – were called into a murder trial. "Will you convict based upon the testimony of a single witness?" the prosecutor asked. The question was put to each of us individually while the defendant was sitting in front of us. She was young and stunningly pretty. Her pale blond hair framed an intelligent face behind large horn-rimmed glasses. WANTED SEX AFTER KILLING, one headline had read in the morning paper.

"The fact that the defendant is a woman, would you hold that against her?"

"The fact that the defendant is *haole* . . ." The word means white.

At the side of the old stone Judiciary Building, there is a porch where we used to stand during breaks in the long process of questioning. Like the building itself, this porch is solid, with a feeling of dark in its corners, and I was standing out there looking at the grass that stretched away to the sidewalk when I saw a friend walk by. She was a former prosecutor and friend of my former in-laws. She was a piece of my past, part of what I was leaving. "Oh," she said when she saw me, "there you are. I heard you were in the jury pool. I hear you keep getting dismissed." She'd been up in the DA's office, visiting her former colleagues.

I shrugged. She knew I was not supposed to discuss what happened in the courtroom.

"Actually, I know the reason you haven't been chosen," she went on recklessly. "Everyone in the office noticed it. You stare. At the defendants. You make too much eye contact."

I said, "Well I'm on my third try."

"Which case?"

She knew the rules. I mumbled, "It's a murder trial."

"*Mon dieu.* The Acker case? She's vicious, that one! She's in prison on the mainland for the same thing!" She held up two fingers. "Two murders at the tender age of eighteen. Her husband's involved too."

"But they don't know she did it."

"Doesn't matter," my friend said. "They'll put her away."

Back inside, I felt queasy. Suppose they asked, during voir dire, if there was any reason I could not be a fair and impartial juror? *Doesn't matter. They'll put her away.* But when my turn came for questioning, the prosecutor had run out of allowable challenges. And that afternoon, with fourteen other people, I stood up shyly, as if I'd been invited out on the floor to dance. I was the second alternate out of three.

4

From the start I kept a notebook, writing something like letters to Maryann Acker as if I thought we might meet someday and talk about her trial. I addressed her directly in my notebook, but sometimes a little angrily. This was because I was sitting in a courtroom in the old stone court-house in Honolulu, where I had lived for long enough to feel I belonged. I was born and bred in Kansas, but I had married the great-grandchild of missionaries who sailed around the horn, disembarked in Honolulu, and stayed. My mother said I had fallen in love with Philip in order to get myself back to Hawaii.

March 18, 1982
When they first read the charges – when they introduced you to us – I could not believe you were a murderer. Your

muumuu is light blue and then that white bodice with its little string at the back, its little drooping tie, gives the impression of something worn in a hospital. In front of you there is a pad of paper and you write at your own pace as if you follow your own thoughts and not the words around us. As if you might be writing to your mother, only what could you say?

Watching Maryann, I kept thinking about my divorce hearing, when Judge Chou, in his black robe, had looked down at me the way Judge Au was looking down at her. I kept remembering the way Philip's lawyer had tried to trick me into admitting that I had no right to child support – "Has he ever supported you?" – and the way I had thought that any minute all of them – the lawyers and the judge – would suddenly confess that the whole thing was a terrible joke. Did I honestly think he wanted the engagement ring back? I remembered the way I had wanted my father, for once, to defend me. I had to remind myself that this was Maryann's trial, not mine.

We had settled ourselves in the jury box, but I kept my eyes on the halo of pale hair around Maryann's face. When the prosecutor stood up to introduce herself, there was a sudden crash of thunder, as if she had planned it for effect. The courtroom got dark. "Jan Futa," she said as the shades at the top of the windows clattered. She raised her voice but we could barely hear all the charges. When she said she was going to produce an eyewitness to the crimes, we leaned forward. Futa was small and delicate, like a ballerina. "The state will prove," she said earnestly, "that, in addition to other crimes, Maryann Acker killed Lawrence Hasker on June 19, 1978." Her long hair was pulled loosely back and tied with a dangling scarf. She wore a severely tailored suit, dark blue with a stripe, and buttoned the jacket all the way to the top. The only decoration she allowed herself was a thin gold bracelet on the right wrist. Always she carried a gold pen in her right hand. It proved, she said, a belief in something unprovable. She believed that if the pen were not there, between index and middle fingers, she would be lost and so, presumably, would be her case.

As she explained the multiple charges – kidnapping, burglary, murder in the first degree – I kept looking at Maryann. There were the heavy glasses, round and dark-rimmed, through which she stared at the table in front of her. When it was her lawyer's turn to address us, the thunder had stopped. "Stephen Hioki," he said, dipping his head and holding his hands behind his back as if he expected someone to put handcuffs around his wrists. He was tall for an Asian man, with bony arms that stuck out of the sleeves of his jacket. What he would show, he said, was the state's lack of evidence. "What the defence intends to show is that Maryann was the companion of a murderer."

Her husband's involved too.

5

The first witness, on that first day of the trial, was another man who had been kidnapped and taken to Hanauma Bay a few days before Larry Hasker was killed. His name was Joe Leach. He said he'd met Maryann at the Garden Bar in the Hilton Hawaiian Village in Waikiki on June 9 and offered to buy her a drink. A margarita, he said it was. He said they'd danced – he didn't remember how many times – and she'd told him her brother was with her and needed a ride. Could he help her out? Then maybe she and Joe could be alone for a while?

Jan Futa pointed at someone in the front of the courtroom. "Is this the man she called her brother?"

Leach said, "That's him," and we took a good look at William Acker. He was thirty-two years old, with a pretty face and a wiry build. Sitting still, he seemed slightly magnetic. But Leach went on testifying and we turned our attention back to the witness stand.

Joe Leach told the court that Maryann had seemed calm as the three of them walked to his car, although he did not know what she was feeling inside. He said William had climbed in back, but Maryann had got in the front. They had used false names. He did not remember what names they had used, but William's hair had been black that night. He said William had been quiet and then he'd pulled a gun and after that it was all obscenities, as if he wanted to make it clear how serious this was going to be. As if he were making monster faces in the dark of the backseat. Leach said he could feel the gun at his hairline. He was trying to follow the directions he was getting, but it was a Honolulu night – stars, the bright lights of Waikiki, the sound of the tide beating against the traffic – and the girl and the man didn't always agree. There was the smell of salt in the air and sweaty flesh, the three of them taking the turns, stopping at the crosswalks in front of red lights. What they told him to do was to drive to Hanauma Bay and he took Kalakaua as far as he could through Waikiki, but the man kept yelling, "He's doing this on purpose, the fuckinshitheel! He's trying to get us lost."

In the front, Maryann tried to calm him down. She turned to the back and said, "I think he's trying his best. Really."

Leach switched course then and drove past the golf course, past Aina Haina, and on along the moon-bright ocean, which stretched forever on the passenger side of the car. The drive took no time. Time had stopped. It stretched then shrank then disappeared. He couldn't describe how uneven it felt. He remembered that he couldn't focus on anything but the two lanes of highway.

At Hanauma, he drove down to the parking lot, but there was a car there so he turned back up toward the highway and, near the top, he put his foot on the brake. For a minute they all sat there. A minute of hard breathing. His wallet had been taken during the drive. It didn't matter. Eighty dollars. His camera too. The girl had taken her pantyhose off, which was strange. Now the man ordered him out of the car. Keep walking. Keep on. Around the bay all that crumbling and all of it steep, Maryann following them down a slope, sometimes slipping. The man told her to use her pantyhose to tie Leach's hands, but she said she couldn't; she said she didn't know how, so the man handed her the gun and told her how to use it. Next he cut the sleeves off Leach's shirt with a knife. He called the knife Justice. Leach was shaking. He watched Maryann holding the gun, and wondered what kind of people would name a knife.

6

Joe Leach had been tied up and gagged and abandoned under the kiawe trees, but he managed to free himself and hobble up to the highway after his captors drove away in his car. He got himself all the way to a police station, which was three miles distant, and someone there took off his gag and listened to what he had to say.

A few days later, Detective Jimon You at the Homicide Division in Honolulu was going through recent police reports, looking for clues to the murder. Hasker was lying in the morgue, where his wounds were being studied. Two wounds. Two bullets. The district attorney wanted an arrest. There had been a string of syndicate killings, including the murder of his own nineteen-year-old son, who had been taken to Waimanalo Beach late one night and shot in the head. The district attorney had campaigned for his office by promising to put an end to crime in Hawaii. He was determined to bring someone to justice.

When Jimon You found the police report filed in Hawaii Kai on June 10, he read it carefully – the details about the sleeves, especially, because Hasker's body had been found near the remnants of another man's shirt. Joe Leach was brought in for questioning. Drawings were made. And now Maryann Acker was on trial and her husband was the prime witness for the state.

All weekend I thought about the trial. At night I dreamed that I was on the witness stand. I was the prosecutor; I was the defendant. I stood to argue and question; I sat to answer and defend. When I was standing I addressed my energies to the twelve people on my right. When I was sitting, I paid close attention to the questions and tried to forget the jury. Number twelve was a blond *haole*, very glamorous. Number eleven was a young Japanese Hawaiian. Number nine, the only *haole* man, kept to himself. Like me, he'd probably lived in the islands for a long time. As a group, we were a fair representation of Hawaii's ethnic mix. The first juror in the top row – number eight – was about fifty, part Hawaiian, with tattoos on his arms. He had several kids, straight black hair. Next a nurse, Japanese, in her forties, who was always making a spectacle of herself. Number four was young and smartly dressed. High-waisted pants, Asian and Portuguese. There are some I've forgotten, but the last one, Mr. Sugai, had answered a question during voir dire by saying he couldn't possibly be impartial because of his beliefs about handguns. "I believe anyone who carries a gun must intend to use it."

That time, the defence had run out of challenges and, like me, Mr. Sugai had to be placed on the jury.

I was friendliest with the other female alternate. We paired off for lunch and often spent recesses together. We were both thinking about what we had heard, although much of it made no sense. Rule 403, Judge Au might say. Evidence was put forward, then dropped. Never mentioned again. The testimonies were confusing and I was glad of this new friend's company although we didn't discuss our thoughts. The previous Friday she had run off for lunch with her husband and I had settled for tacos and a plastic bowl of refried beans on the courthouse grass. Two blocks away, at the end of the street, I could see a four-masted schooner, all rigging and lines against the sky. At the other end of the street, I could see the white columns of the palace, home of Hawaii's short-lived monarchy. I was thinking about that morning's evidence. We'd spent an hour looking at photographs and diagrams.

There were colour pictures of Larry Hasker's body at the murder site and at the morgue. What affected me most were the clear plastic bags, which held a red plaid flannel shirt, brown corduroy pants, underwear, and a pair of rubber slippers. After four years, those objects seemed too intimate to be looked at by us, and I was glad they were not taken out of the bags.

It was easy to walk down to the palace grounds, where the Royal Hawaiian band plays at noon on Fridays. A nice hula, and Healani Miller singing "Kaulana o Hilo" to the strains of the band. When our last king, Kalakaua, was crowned here in 1883, he allowed the hula to be danced for the first time since its suppression by the missionaries. Now, when the band played "Aloha 'Oe," everyone stood up, even the tourists.

Then, back in the courtroom, the girl who had gone for a walk four years before told about finding the body, except that, as she spoke, it was no longer "the body" but "him." She kept saying "him." Next, Larry Hasker's father was called to the stand with something unnamable in his face. Suddenly I wanted to jump up and grab Maryann. She stared at the father and at Larry Hasker's best friend and at the girl who found the body. She stared at the sister, whose name was Kimberly. These were clear, detached stares with an ounce of fuck you in them.

March 22

Today, when Larry's father came in, Mr. Hasker Senior, when he glanced at you and then sat staring, only pulling his eyes away when the prosecutor demanded his attention, I thought I could actually see the thin, transparent membrane that separates the accused of this world from the accusers. As Mr. Hasker spoke about his son, I wanted to throw myself at you. I could see your face pushed down, my hands around your neck. I could see your tongue sticking out, your legs kicking. Sullen, brutal bitch.

It had never occurred to me before that the reason we kill murderers is that they have this effect on us – of making us murderous.

7

On Tuesday, March 24, my daughter Esta came into town with me because Philip was going to pick her up at the courthouse. We had time to go into the lobby for a snack and, while we were standing there, Maryann was brought through – the accused – passing near enough that we could have touched her.

We bought a muffin and a bread pudding from the blind woman who worked the coin machine and microwave oven and kept tabs on all the ice cream, drinks, candy, and snacks. When someone asked for a newspaper, she said that they were all gone. I thought: blind justice. Then I remembered the knife. I introduced Esta to my alternate-friend, who promised to have lunch with me later, when we would sit at Heidi's, outside in the cold wind. But for most of the day we would listen to Maryann's husband, who was the prime witness for the state. For most of the day he would be a little cocky, but charming. "This time I must get it right. I want to tell the truth the truth the truth." High-strung and eerily sexy, William Acker kept looking at us and smiling. Spousal immunity is part of American law. Husbands and wives cannot testify against each other, being considered incapable of objectivity. But in Hawaii this law had been overturned the year before, possibly, I thought, to catch Maryann.

The prosecutor began by establishing facts. William was born in Illinois in 1950 and grew up in Paramount, California. He'd met Maryann Bray in Phoenix in April 1978 at Arizona Hardware, where she was an accounts receivable clerk. He was just out of jail, recently paroled to his sister, and he got a job working in the warehouse. "Correct?"

"Yes, ma'am."

"And what were you doing there?"

"Shipping clerk."

I tried to imagine being eighteen and seeing William saunter over to my desk. I'm at work, my head bent over some receipts, and I look up and there is that off-centre smile, that sloping hello. I could imagine dropping my pencil and hoping my hair was okay. I remembered Philip in his checked jacket the first time I saw him in a bar. He was standing by the door, using the pay phone, and my heart almost stopped.

"When is it that you were married?"

"April 29, that same month."

"And why did you and your wife leave Arizona?"

"Lot of bill collectors knocking on the door." William grinned.

"What kind of bills?"

"She had this bank card that enabled her to write cheques, buy things, you know." He shrugged. "There was nothing in the bank, but it was a guaranteed card. Even if you perhaps didn't have money in the bank, you could still use it." William made me want to take him home and feed him a steak.

"Now how did you buy the tickets to come to Hawaii?" Jan Futa's face was alive with quizzical looks.

"With that guaranteed card."

"And what is it that you brought with you?"

"Luggage and a gun and a knife and things that belonged to us."

Keeping her head down, Maryann made notes on a piece of paper and never once looked at the man she must once have loved. The prosecutor took William through their first hours in Hawaii, when one of "the luggages" was lost. "What was in that piece of lost luggage?"

"The knife. Also a .38 revolver."

"Can you describe it?"

"It was a snub-nosed Smith & Wesson."

"And the knife?"

"Yes, ma'am. Justice."

"So you got that piece of lost luggage back." Futa was twirling the gold pen between her fingers like a tiny wand. "And after you moved to the Makiki Arms here in Honolulu, what were you doing to make a living?" The apartment Maryann shared with her husband in 1978 was just around the corner from the place my brother had lived with his wife and baby. I knew the neighbourhood: Punchbowl, the ancient crater, and the Chinese cemetery I used to walk around when I was fourteen, looking at the narrow stones with their calligraphy.

"She made me feel pretty bad. We didn't have nothing to eat and no job. So we discussed robberies." William was oddly childlike. "Yes, ma'am. I wanted to rob people who wanted to buy narcotics, kind of like a sting or a burn. The reason is that's what I wanted to do."

"And why is it that you chose that plan?"

"Because it's pretty safe in two ways. It was easy to live with. And, you know, plus what are they going to tell the cops: I wanted to buy some dope and he ripped me off?"

"And when you say easy to live with, what do you mean?"

"It's hard for me to pull robberies, you know. It's hard to initiate force or violence." The prosecutor was showing us William's soft side. "I didn't want to influence her; I didn't want her to influence me. It had to be right. And she convinced me that it could be right to go ahead."

Jan Futa asked what happened when Maryann met Joe Leach in the Garden Bar and William smiled. "I romanced some chick walking by and went and danced while they were dancing."

The prosecutor twirled her pen. "And how was Maryann acting toward Joe in the bar?"

"Like he had a play coming."

"What do you mean?" She tilted her head.

"Romance. Without getting gross, that's the best way I can say it."

We were not allowed to write in the courtroom, so I made notes during recess, or after we had quit for the day. I sat under a tree. Or I wrote in the car. I'd feed the meter another quarter and write before I drove home. Maybe I did this because I wanted to understand Maryann. Maybe that's why I directed the notes to her. *If you discussed robberies beforehand* . . . Or maybe I liked the feel of the pen in my hand – like the prosecutor – the feel of importance, as if the case depended on me. I was the daughter of a lawyer. I'd spent summers working in his office and hundreds of hours watching Perry Mason win cases on TV. William had two criteria for his victims. They should be involved with drugs and they should be tourists. Hasker and Leach were both residents, but William said Maryann had chosen them. "We argued a little bit."

I knew the prosecutor would be easy on William because he was her witness. In fact, by the time Jan Futa had moved on to the kidnapping and murder of Larry Hasker, William was almost enjoying himself. "Well I thought, yeah, we'll rob him. It's something he did or something he said that let me know that he was tied in with nobody, you know. I was kind of playing with him, you know. But I had told Maryann if I leave, that means no. And I left, I told him I got to go take care of something."

"Did Maryann leave with you?"

"No. She met up with me later. She couldn't be rude and just leave. Then later we ran into him again at another disco . . ." William paused and put his head back as if he could find the name on the ceiling. For a long minute he stared up and we waited. "To me it seemed like he was on his way to find us and he bought us some drinks, flashed big money, you know, and I told him, I said maybe he and Maryann could get together."

"And what was your impression as to how Maryann was feeling?"

"She wanted to rob him from the beginning. Even we argued when she came back to meet me. Wow, that guy had money, you should have stung him."

With Joe Leach, they had gone directly to Hanauma Bay, but they took Hasker to their own apartment first, as if they were all going to sit down together and have a friendly drink. William said he had second thoughts at that point. "Because when we rob him, then he can know where we live." So, while Larry sat in the living room, William and Maryann closed the door to the bedroom and had another argument. I tried to picture it – the cheap furniture, the length of blue nylon cord on the unmade bed, the gun on a water-stained dresser. William said the knife was in Maryann's purse. "That's where it always was. That was her role."

Back in the living room, William tied Larry up with the blue nylon cord. "We had both taken our shirts off. You know, it was hot. And I tied him behind his back, put his shirt on him, and told him . . . oh, he didn't think, you know, when I first pulled down on him, he didn't think he was going to be robbed. He said, Oh come on, man, or something like that. This can't be real. I assured him it was and put his shirt over him and told him to play drunk, man, in case the neighbours were out and about, like I'm helping him to his car."

This time Maryann drives. Another difference. She drives to Hasker's building and then goes up in the elevator while the two men wait in the car. I pictured her at the door, clutching the key. She must have been nervous. Hasker and his sister lived on the tenth floor of a high-rise near the university. It's a crowded building. Maryann lets herself in very quietly. She listens. What if the sister is home? On the other side of the room there is a bureau and in it the book where Hasker hides his money. She crosses the floor and takes it out of the top drawer and shakes it, picking up $400 in twenties. Then she grabs a tape recorder. Hasker has asked her to bring him a joint. Next, back in the car, he's smoking the joint and William's holding the gun when Maryann says, "Let's drive him to the bay where the other guy was."

"Did you or Maryann smoke any dope?"

"No. I think he finished it before we . . . I think he was already *pau*." Finished. In the courtroom, there was a communal intake of breath. Pidgin is our trademark, our shared code. William was one of us.

8

It was King Kamehameha who proclaimed the first law against murder in Hawaii, and he used witnesses to test innocence or guilt. This happened almost a century before King Kalakaua wrote the national anthem and allowed his people to revert to the old ways by performing the hula. First, Kamehameha united the islands, murdering thousands in the process. Next, he established a system of taxation for his large kingdom that recompensed governors, district chiefs, and village headmen. If there was a disagreement – since all the ancient *kapus* were in place and the number of criminal offences was vast, Kamehameha was the final arbiter. In front of his grass house he gathered witnesses in a circle while the accused was told to hold his hands over a calabash of water. If the hands trembled, the person was guilty.

That was the start of our monarchy, which was conquered in 1893, when the American plantation owners brought out their guns and flags and took over.

9

On the fourth day of the trial, William described the murder. "He said he wanted to use the bathroom. His words were 'I want to take a piss.'"

"And where were you at the time?"

"I walked around him, got in the driver's seat, put on the gloves."

"And where was Maryann?"

"She was standing on the passenger side of the door with the gun."

"Then what happened?"

"She shot him, shot him."

"How many times?"

"Three."

"Where was Larry when she shot him?"

"He had finished taking a piss. He zipped up. And he

turned toward her a little bit. Not to jump on her, nothing like that. In fact, he said, I'm going to fall. I told him, I know it, you're going to fall. That way you won't know which way we go."

"When you heard the shots, what did you see him do?"

"Like he was hit, like he turned and fell. He fell down where he was going to walk. He fell down, he fell down there."

"What did Maryann do after she fired the gun?"

"She just stood there. It was not what she did, it was what I did. I reached over and opened the door and told her, Get in the car. Yelled at her. Got nervous, real scared. She did it. She sat in the car. I told her, What the fuck did you do that for, you know, why? The answer was strange."

Jan Futa did not ask William what the answer was. She did not ask him why it was strange. She asked, "What did you do?"

"Turned the lights off and on trying to start the car. I forgot how to start the car. My mind was blown, it was unreal. Finally got the car started and headed in the wrong direction, not the way I wanted to go."

"And what was Maryann doing?"

"Looking at the bullets, throwing them out the window."

"Can you describe how Maryann appeared to you at that time?"

"Like I do this every day, real calm. Like: You're the macho man, what's happening with you, you know, wow. Like I misled her, like I wasn't the person she thought I was, trying to make me feel bad."

After the wrong direction and panic, Maryann and William switched places so that she could drive. This happened, William said, at Sandy Beach, where he wanted to throw the gun out but she wouldn't let him. Instead he took it back to the apartment and decided to hide it. "I made up my mind to leave. I was scared, I was scared." He was trying to go to the laundry room to use the phone, "But she wanted to get down."

"She wanted to what?"

"She wanted to get down. Go to bed. I told her, I made a statement to her, What? She goes, I was blown, you know, I was freaked out." Then he added, shaking his head, "I couldn't believe it," and looked over at us.

William said he went down to the laundry room to use the phone and hide the gun. "I was calling the airlines to leave, finding out information when the flights leave. But I didn't get the right information so I just stayed there and walked around. I was trying to think, trying to get a grip on my thoughts, what to do, you know. And why, I wanted whys answered. I wanted a lot of things answered. And I couldn't answer them, only Maryann could. So I was, you know, trying to get back to reality. You know.

I'm sorry I had to rob. I got back on the phone. And she tapped me on the shoulder. She says, You're leaving. . . . She said things like, Don't abandon me."

Listening to William, I thought of the terror I felt when Philip left. It was summer. My father had died in June and now it was July. I had a two-year-old and a four-year-old and no real qualifications for earning a living. It was a terrible time. I was mad with shock and jealousy. I was heart-broken, half-sick and crazy. I was twenty-eight years old and for the very first time I was in charge of my life.

"It was just unreal. And it was just real bad." Listening to William now.

"And then what happened?"

"So she realized I was just freaked out. And I loved Maryann at that time, I really did. So I made arrangements."

That morning, the same morning of Larry Hasker's death, they left Hawaii and flew to Los Angeles. William told about not sitting together on the plane, about what names they had used, and how she had brought the gun when he told her not to bring it, how she had packed it in a red plastic container, how he had tried to get away from her, going to a motel and checking in while she waited for the luggage. Later, though, she knocked on his door. She was holding the gun. He said by then he was really afraid.

He said, "I'm going. That gun is all you." He said, "I hid that gun a lot from her that night."

"So from there you and Maryann were together still? Where did you go?"

"Up north."

We heard a long sigh, as if the defence attorney had already exhausted himself. Then Stephen Hioki stood up slowly, as if gathering his strength. When he said he wanted to make an objection with regard to the next area of questioning, I remembered the words I had heard on the stone lanai. *She's in prison on the mainland for the same thing.* Was that the area of questioning Futa was about to raise?

Judge Au called both lawyers to the bench, where we couldn't hear what they were saying. Hioki kept gesturing, flailing his arms and hands. Judge Au was shaking his head and Futa was standing on her tiptoes, peering over the bench as if she needed to make herself seen. I thought about Larry Hasker, whose death seemed to be more important than his life. I thought of him standing on the rough hillside, the moon high above him, washing everything in its unhealthy light. Below, the ocean pulling out and out. Nearby, Leach's torn shirt, grey with a black design. He would fall very close to it. He would swallow the water and moon and the promises of these strangers. Swallow everything, his entire life.

IO

When I was still a child and my father was still teaching at the local law school, there was a mock trial for the students and my father asked me to play the role of a witness. I was twelve or thirteen and I was going to prove myself. I was given a piece of paper with the details of a car accident: something about a goat. Now I started thinking about the goat and that long-ago mock trial while I was sitting in the Honolulu jury box, waiting for the judge and the lawyers to finish their bench conference. First I was thinking about Larry and his death. Then I thought of William and how hard it must be to remember pertinent facts. Then I remembered the goat. It seemed to me that I was the driver, that I was the one who had killed the goat, although I was, of course, too young to drive. There were other witnesses. Not false witnesses but fake witnesses. Mock witnesses. They came out of imaginary houses along the imaginary road and described the imaginary scene they had not witnessed. They did not even imagine they had witnessed it, but the students were told to imagine not only that they had done so but that the goat had really existed and that the farmer who had owned the goat and even perhaps loved the goat was suing the driver of the car for damages.

This was my chance to get it right. I dressed the way my father told me to dress and worked hard to remember the condition of the road and whether the headlights were working, although it was hard because I have an active imagination and sometimes I add on to things. I said the goat was white and that one of his horns was gone and even as I sat there in front of those Kansas students, I couldn't remember whether I'd read that in the notes or whether I'd seen it in my mind while I was reading. Now, thinking back, I was not absolutely sure I'd run over the goat. What I did remember was that every one of the witnesses told a different story.

I held on to that thought when Jan Futa resumed her questioning and William said he had wanted Maryann to go home. "She kept making me feel that nothing I do was right." I held on to that thought when he described how they hitchhiked north, then how they suddenly changed direction, getting a ride from a young man whose name was spelled out for the court. C-e-s-a-r-i-o A-r-a-u-z-a. He was driving a Chevrolet Blazer with a stick shift, which William said he did not know how to drive. He said Maryann took the wheel so Arauza could have a nap.

"Mr. Acker, can you describe Cesario Arauza?"

"Yeah, he's bigger. A lot bigger. Mexican American."

"Now, did anything happen on the way down south?"

"With Cesario? Yeah, he was murdered."

Somewhere close to L.A., near a cloverleaf, they stopped at a restaurant and gas station and William went in to order some takeout food. He was hungry, and Arauza had given him money so that he could eat. Ten dollars, he thought it was. While William waited for the food, Maryann said she wanted to take Arauza's car. "She said he was making a pass at her. Let's take this creep's car and leave him here." William said he argued against it, but finally he took her to the public restroom and gave her the unloaded gun. She spent a few minutes alone in there, he said, and then got back in the car and drove off with Arauza, who looked back at William through the rear window as if he couldn't believe his luck. William forgot about the food and walked to the highway, planning to hitchhike alone, but twenty minutes later Maryann picked him up. "Twenty minutes. Or it might have been longer. It felt longer to me." He checked the gun and saw that it was loaded. Smelled it. "I didn't think it had been fired at that point." Maryann said she had left Arauza at an on-ramp, that taking the car had been easy.

They used Arauza's car in three more robberies. For a night or two they slept in it. Then, in Long Beach, they rented a room in a motel and Maryann wanted to "flame" the car. William said she went out to the parking lot and he waited for her, but she didn't come back. He said, "So I got up on the roof and I saw some squad cars. More than one. And I felt that she got arrested. I went back to the room to look for the gun. I panicked. I packed everything up in a flight bag, but I couldn't find the gun. I threw all her shit on the floor, out of her purse, looking for it. And I went upstairs by the phone. And the cops came. A lot of cop cars drove up and I saw Maryann in one of them." William stayed hidden and watched as the room was searched. When everyone had gone, he left on foot, taking a Greyhound bus to Yuma, where he called Bert Bray, Maryann's father, from the bus station. "He told me that, 'Man, you got my daughter in trouble. She's in jail.'"

Charged with murder.

At Bert Bray's urging, William agreed to turn himself in. "To clear things up. Because of the bullets that were used. He said hollow points, and we didn't have no hollow points except for five that came with the gun that we already used practising in Arizona."

Remember the goat, I told myself, because William couldn't remember whether he had called Los Angeles or the Yuma police. Or maybe Maryann's father had driven him to the police station, he wasn't sure. What he was sure about was the bullets. Hollow points. He said they had never used them. Later he said they had hollow-point bullets in Arizona when they were practising with the gun. Remember the goat, because Leach had said William instructed Maryann about the gun, telling her how to use it.

II

In the spring of 1979, a few months after Cesario Arauza's murder and a few weeks after William had been convicted, Detective Jimon You received a phone call from the Los Angeles sheriff's office. He was told that a man in custody there had information about a murder in Hawaii. William may have been hoping that his offer of information would lighten the California sentence, which he had not yet received, but perhaps Detective You had no qualms about that. He flew to L.A. to interview William as soon as he could book a flight. "They took the victim to Hanauma Bay," he wrote in his subsequent report, "and his wife took the victim into the bushy area. The guy then said that he heard three shots; his wife returned and he asked her if the guy was all right and she replied, 'No, he's dead.' The guy also added that his wife used a .38-calibre revolver with some of the bullets being hollow points."

William signed a plea agreement with Charles Marsland, the DA whose son had been shot on a beach in Waimanalo, not far from Hanauma Bay. "You know," William said, speaking of Hasker's murder, "it went over and over and over and over and over. And it was a senseless thing."

In his California trial, William had acted as his own counsel. Now, when Jan Futa asked him if he had researched California law, he said, "Where murder is concerned, that's right."

And why had he decided to take responsibility for the Arauza murder? Why had he pleaded *nolo contendere*?

"Because in California they have what's called felony murder rule. When there is a crime or when two people do a crime or three and as a result of that somebody's shot and killed, stabbed and killed, hung, whatever – when they're killed, each defendant is charged with murder and held responsible."

That afternoon, around three o'clock, Stephen Hioki began his cross-examination of William. Advancing and retreating between his chair and the witness stand, he seemed tense and unprepared. After noting that William was twenty-eight and Maryann eighteen when they married and that they had known each other less than two months when Larry Hasker was shot, he said, "Now, isn't it true that prior to the marriage Maryann was a fairly close follower of the Mormon Church?"

William said, "No, that's not true."

Mormon. Everyone in the courtroom must have made something of that, one of the biggest Mormon temples in the world is on O'ahu. There might easily have been a Mormon on the jury. My own great-grandmother was a convert, although my family is still ashamed of her. Heaven. The Second Coming. Prophecies. The Mormons are zealots. But Hioki was beating a fast retreat. Did William recall speaking to a detective in L.A.? Did he recall saying that they had found Cesario Arauza's Blazer on the side of a California highway?

"Initially, yes."

"So you lied?" Hioki was clenching and unclenching his fists.

"Definitely. I made statements, you know, there was a lot of statements made. And sometimes memory was better and sometimes it wasn't. But going back to the initial statement," William continued calmly, "I lied tremendously. That's when I was going to fight the robberies and murders." He paused. "I didn't know about the murder. I mean, I knew, but I did not . . . I was positive it wasn't ours because of the hollow points that killed him. We didn't have any hollow-point bullets. But I was going to evade the robberies, you know. And I talked pretty good . . ."

"And you were going to fight them by lying?"

"Well, a convict or a criminal doesn't tell the police the truth."

Someone laughed. Someone in the courtroom.

Had William ever bought bullets at GEMs in Honolulu?

"Yes."

"Isn't it true that you purchased these bullets for the purpose of sending a bullet a day to a neighbour in Arizona to intimidate him?"

"That's what I told the detective, but it's not true."

"Hadn't these people accused you of stealing their .38-calibre revolver?"

"I heard mention of that, yeah. But the fact is Maryann stole that gun. She knew where it was."

Hioki introduced two letters and asked William to examine them. "Do you recognize the handwriting, Mr. Acker?" He was making himself sound forceful, as he had probably been trained to do in law school.

"It appears to be mine unless somebody's a real good forger." This time everyone laughed.

Hioki read the letters aloud. To Bert Bray, Maryann's father, William had written: "'What can I say? I got what I had coming. I tried a twisted plan concerning Hawaii, hoping they would offer Maryann deals. But instead, I will catch the Hawaii charges. In fact, I've already told the Attorney General I would cop to the Hawaiian affairs . . .'" Hioki asked him to explain.

"I believe," William said, scratching his neck, "this was when I was going to cop to everything. I might have told this to Bert Bray. But I also bullshitted Bert Bray a whole lot because he did me too."

The second letter was to Maryann, although William had addressed it to Free, which he said was his name for her "because of her ability to stay out of jail at that time." He had written: "'Honey, I couldn't tell you then, nor can I fully explain now. But the two heavy things that went down were mine to take. I will explain when I can, sister of mine in the Randanian way.'" Hioki paused. He said, "What did you mean by that?"

William said, "It's a step beyond Ayn Rand. It's taking her a step further than she goes. It's a philosophy."

"Doesn't this philosophy basically mean you look out for yourself first and foremost?"

"No. It basically means you are yourself."

Hioki closed his eyes. Then he opened them and returned to the letter. But I was watching his narrow face, his chin like a spoon, his eyes humourless. He was shaking the letter as if it contained loose dirt. "You indicated that as far as you know, it was Maryann who killed Mr. Arauza, is that right?"

"Yes."

"Isn't it true that the day after Mr. Arauza was killed you told a Mr. Raymond Guillen that the orange and red spot on your pants was from the blood of a man you had just killed the day before?"

"No. That's not true."

Hioki dropped the question and we were never to hear another word about the pants or the blood. When he jumped back to Phoenix and asked why William and Maryann had left – was it to evade William's parole officer? – the question was stricken. Once, William corrected him bluntly. "No, no. Read my lips." When Hioki mistakenly referred to William as Mr. Leach, William said flatly, "I'm not Mr. Leach." Hioki said, "Sorry. I'm sorry." But William was becoming belligerent. When asked about the Hasker murder, he told Hioki they'd never gone to Larry's apartment. Then he said they went to Larry's apartment first, after the bar, and then to their own. Then he said, "You're not listening to me. We went to our apartment, the gun was pulled on him, then we went to his apartment because he said he had cocaine and money."

"Okay," said Hioki. "Okay."

"You understand that?"

"Okay."

"I told you. Now, listen to me real carefully, watch my mouth."

But Steven Hioki did not look at William; he looked down at his notes. He said, "You indicated during direct examination that you represented yourself in the California case, is that correct?"

"Yes I did."

"And you researched the area of law concerning murder, is that right?"

"And robberies."

"And based on your research you decided that you should plead guilty because under California law you were responsible for that particular incident, isn't that right?"

"Just as responsible."

Suddenly, Maryann's lawyer slipped out an invisible knife. "And can you explain, Mr. Acker, why you were sentenced to life without parole?"

Futa leapt to her feet. "Objection!"

The judge sounded alarmed. "I'll see counsel in chambers," he announced, banging his gavel. Then he called a recess, telling us to disregard Hioki's remark. But what did Hioki want us to know about William? That he had nothing to lose, so he would swear to anything? But why not this: that he had nothing to lose, but also nothing to gain?

Life without parole.

The point was not to take everything personally, but I got stuck on the thought of my great-grandfather, who ran off to Yuma and tried to start a new life. He'd left his wife and children. Everything. Burned the last bridge. Now I began to think of William as my unfortunate relative. My history.

I went straight home that night and Michael was there, waiting. We had started our new life together with his five-month teaching visit to Hawaii. That night, and every night, I went home to Michael and Esta and Kristin and whatever had happened in their day. I went home to the dog and cat, to the house, to the garden that needed attention, to a dinner that had to be made. I went home to the newspaper, which was full of holes, since Michael cut out any articles about the trial. I was careful not to listen to the radio or watch the news on TV. But there were voices in my head still talking to me. I'd be standing over Esta, watching her do her homework, and I'd remember some line of questioning: "And after the robbery of Mr. Leach, did she want sex then?"

I'd be standing in the kitchen, putting the dishes away, and I'd hear William's answer. "Are you trying to exploit Maryann's sex life or mine?" which was nothing compared to my confusion about the gun. Who had it? Who hid it? He took a walk first or maybe he didn't. He made a phone call while he was hiding it. Or he made it later. He was scared. "I didn't want nothing to do with the bitch." But he bought two tickets. They left together. They had the .38 called Little John and a knife named Justice and five days later in California, Cesario Arauza was killed. I couldn't talk about these things that went round and round in my head. I was waiting for Maryann to be called to the stand. But what could she possibly say after everything we had heard?

12

March 26

You are as pale as the moon. Today you will take the
stand. You will be a surprise package presented to us by
your lawyer. But first we must finish with your husband.
"The night you robbed Mr. Leach, did Maryann wear
her glasses?" "No. She usually wore contacts then. Oh,
Maryann could doll herself up. She didn't need a disguise.
She would just change her looks."

Apparently you have only two outfits, the soft muumuu
and this white dress with a tight, white jacket. The dress
has an odd strap in back, visible through the light mate-
rial of the jacket. Who chooses your clothes? Who cuts your
hair and buys your makeup? The shoes are so high that

you tip forward on the platform heels. Each time you come in from recess, you cross the room slowly, as if you are walking through water, focusing on the destination of your chair.

Kristin was in the courtroom that morning. Among the rows of observers, I could pick out her small, familiar face. At lunchtime, my alternate-friend and her daughter went with us to a restaurant. Kristin said, "Of course, she did it, didn't she?" and "He's awful!" meaning Hioki. "Brown jacket! Green pants!"

That afternoon, Hioki called Maryann to the stand at last. He looked like he wanted to carry her up in his arms, but that wasn't necessary; she swam through the distance between her table and the judge's high bench. And then I heard her voice, which was soft and low-pitched.

"Was the knife in your purse?" Hioki asked.

"I don't recall."

"What name were you using that night?"

"I'm not sure."

On the stand she seemed not so much frail as non-existent.

I looked around now, trying to find members of Maryann's family. If I were on trial, my mother would be here, I thought. She'd bring me things to read in prison. She'd bring me books and soap. And if my father were alive, he'd be here defending me. Although he had told me time and again that if I ever got put in jail he would make no attempt to bail me out.

"Why was it that you came here?"

"I wanted to come and I came with him."

"Who named the knife Justice? Did you?"

"No, I did not. Bill did."

When Maryann went over the details of the Leach robbery, her voice was a whisper. Her face was bloodless. It was William who stole the gun. It was William who decided to rob Mr. Leach. When they drove to Hanauma, it was William who pointed the way. "And then Bill had him stop and Mr. Leach got out. They walked off the side of the road down the ravine. Then Bill called me and asked me to hold the gun while he tied Mr. Leach up."

"Did he instruct you on how to use the gun?"

"I don't believe so." Maryann was not going to help herself.

Hioki asked her about the Hasker murder. He said, "Where were you, Maryann?"

"In the car."

"Which seat?"

"The driver's seat."

"Then what happened?"

"Then I heard gunshots."

"Do you recall how many?"

"Two." She said William came back to the car, told her to move over, and then drove off in the wrong direction. When she asked him what had happened he said it was just something he had to do. He stopped at a restaurant. Maryann did not want to eat. He took her home and went off to park the car. When he came back he said he wanted to leave and went down to the laundry room.

Then the Arauza story. William was in the backseat. He told Arauza to stop the car and get out. They went down a slope. She heard a shot. Again William said it was something he had to do. She made it sound almost boring.

When Hioki asked her about being Mormon, she said, "I was a Sunday-school teacher."

"Did you terminate that work prior to coming to Hawaii?"

"It was causing a lot of problems between Bill and I. He strongly objected. And because of him there were questions raised in my mind about the validity of my religion."

"Now, did you hear Mr. Acker use the word *Randanian*?"

"Yes."

"To your knowledge, who created this philosophy?"

"Bill did. He was going by the philosophy of the author Ayn Rand." Maryann was wearing the white dress and her pale hair fell around her face. Every minute or so, she reached up to adjust her glasses, as if they did not fit her well. "It's ego-centred. Look out for yourself only. It's atheist and very self-centred." There was a darker line where her hair was parted, so the blond wasn't natural. I wondered how she managed that in prison. She wore only a little blush and pink lipstick. When she spoke, I watched her stillness. The relationship – it was strained. Decisions – he made them all.

"Now during the time that you were in Hawaii, did you experience any type of fear of bodily harm?" Hioki edged his way toward the witness stand, as if to remind her that the male body can be threatening.

"Yes, I did." There had been an argument in the apartment. There were a lot of arguments, but after one of them William pointed the gun at her and the gun went off. "The bullet went right by my face."

I was listening for emotion. But there wasn't any.

13

Day six and I was no longer an alternate. Juror number three was ill. For five days I had felt marginal, but this was better. Our vote had to be unanimous, so mine would matter. I would listen harder. We'd had a three-day break and Jan Futa was looking refreshed. She started her cross-examination of Maryann by asking about Yuma, Arizona, where Maryann had finished high school. Then she asked about Phoenix, where Maryann had gone by herself at the age of seventeen. Why had she left home? Was there trouble with her parents? Wasn't she running with a fast crowd? Wasn't she frustrated by the smallness of Yuma? Only a few months after leaving home, hadn't she met William and married him? "Would you really have considered yourself a good Mormon, Ms. Acker, before you met William?" The prosecutor's questions were nicely connected, like a narrative, as if she had rehearsed them many times.

"Yes," said Maryann. Cigarettes, coffee, alcohol. Everything had started with William. I tried to remember if anyone had ever affected me in quite that way. I've gone down a few dark paths, but my parents were temperate. I learned to drink and smoke at home. Our Episcopalian household had no room for purity.

Then Futa asked about the quick departure for Hawaii and the decision to stay. "You cashed in the return tickets that you and Bill had shortly after you got here, isn't that true?"

"Yes."

"And you used that cash to live on?" Futa wanted us to know about Maryann's finances, to remember that she had charged two roundtrip airline tickets, that she was a girl who made decisions. "And you had your bank card at that time, right? But you didn't leave Bill?" She wanted us to know that Maryann had whatever it took to escape, that Maryann had used her maiden name to rent the apartment and later she'd used it to pawn stolen things. She'd used her charms to entrap two men. She'd held the gun on Joe Leach and driven Larry Hasker's car. She was steering us toward what my father would have called a

foregone conclusion, that Maryann was a willing partici-
pant in the kidnappings, the robberies. That the murder
was hers.

The questions came faster and faster. "Did you hear
any talking before you heard the shots?" "How long after
you lost sight of them did you hear the shots?" "And how
quickly did one shot follow the other?" "Was it like bang
bang or was it bang, bang, or how was it?"

When Futa brandished some papers, Judge Au peered
over his glasses. "What does it purport to be? A letter?"

The prosecutor moved over to the witness stand. She
smiled up at the judge and asked Maryann to identify the
handwriting on the pages. Then she began to read with
the hint of a smirk in her voice: "'Honey, please don't blame
yourself for what happened to us,'" she read. There was a
long look at Maryann, a raising of eyebrows. "'You tried
to keep me from it,'" she went on, "'and I was fully aware
of what could happen, but I didn't want to leave.'" There
was the foregone conclusion again. "Did you write that?"

"Yes."

"Did you also go on to write, 'I also realized, though,
that this wouldn't have happened if I wasn't with you. I
suppose I should have thought more of that also. I'm sorry
sweetheart. I love you. I know that we will once again be
together. Honey, this is what I want.'"

The letter had been written while Maryann was in prison in California, waiting for her trial there. It crossed my mind that she might have wanted her husband's help, might have pretended loyalty out of fear, but Futa spun around to look at us indignantly. "When you were with Mr. Leach, you were frightened, is that correct?"

"Yes."

"And do you think that when you were going through your role of enticing him, so to speak, do you think that he knew you were frightened? And with Mr. Hasker? Would it be fair to say that with both men you played your roles with them very well?"

Hioki objected that this was argumentative.

"Do you feel you were doing a good job of leading them on?" Futa continued. And of course by the end of it, when she asked, "Ms. Acker, have you played other roles in your life?" we had heard the point underlined. Maryann could look at us with her blue, blue eyes and say anything and almost be believed.

14

Eighteen years later I would find the yellow notebook. Yellow with a red spine, as if designed to be noticed. I would find it under a pile of papers in a cupboard in Toronto, forgotten, like the trial. In the back of the notebook were the clippings that Michael had cut out of the newspapers on the last day.

"Acker, 22, showed little emotion as the verdicts were announced, but her cheeks appeared flushed and her head dropped slightly when the murder conviction was read."

"The circuit court jurors who convicted Maryann Acker of murder yesterday felt that it really didn't matter if she fired the fatal shot. . . ."

"During the seven-day trial here, the prosecution's key witness was William Acker, who also was charged with the same Hawaii crimes, except for the murder. As part of a plea agreement, he pleaded guilty to robbing Hasker and agreed to testify against his ex-wife. In exchange, the prosecution will dismiss the other counts."

There was the headline that read, WANTED SEX AFTER KILLING and this:

"The jurors had deliberated an hour and 45 minutes."

For eighteen years I had tried not to think about my part in Maryann's life. For ten of those years I had suffered a depression so dark that at times it swallowed me. I'd become fixated on certain things: Death. Murder. My incapacity to befriend. The way I run away from things. I had moved to Canada, trying to leave myself behind. Maybe I had done it: lost myself. Now I turned the pages of the yellow notebook and looked at the dates. What surprised me is that I had kept writing even after the end.

April 5
It's over. Everyone at work knows I was on the jury and, of course, when I saw co-workers during the trial I

laughed it off. I didn't mind describing your features and mannerisms, but I honestly didn't want to feel influenced. I wanted to decide for myself. I wanted to know I could decide. During voir dire I had said yes when asked whether I was willing to pass judgment on another human being. If I cannot judge her, I'd thought, who can?

I had imagined myself sitting in the jury room, which would look like the jury room in *Twelve Angry Men*. Everyone would be voting to convict and I would express my reasonable doubt. William was serving life without parole. His testimony had been elaborate, full of details, like my story of the one-horned goat. Was it believable? William had a past and he had been cocky, pleased with himself. Yet the state had taken him at his word.

In a murder trial, the vote must be unanimous. As a fully fledged member of the jury now, I had to be sure. I had to weigh Maryann's innocent face, her soft hair, her voice. I had to weigh her Mormon childhood, her devout parents, the strict upbringing she must have received. I knew about teenage rebellion. I knew about trying to please a man and being afraid.

Was Maryann Acker a killer?

It was time to decide.

It had become our routine, since Michael had come to live with us, to drive together through the long grasses of

Kawanui Marsh, out to the highway, and across the astonishing Pali, where King Kamehameha cornered the O'ahu warriors and forced them over the edge. An image of warriors floating downward through the mist haunts everyone who crosses, it is so established in the histories, so sung about, so simultaneously mourned and praised, this final conquest that united all of the Hawaiian Islands. It is Kamehameha's gold statue that stands in front of the courthouse, covered in leis.

It was our practice to cross this high place, usually at a bumper-to-bumper crawl, listening to music, talking: the politics of the English department, the trial, and plans for our life together in Canada. But on that last day of the trial, something was wrong with the dog, an unbeautiful cockapoo, black and ungroomed.

We were a few minutes ahead of schedule. We had time to drop him at the vet's before we started across the mountains for town. But the dog had no appointment and we were told to take him back home.

It was here that a five-minute break in my life changed everything in Maryann's.

TORONTO

15

The morning I found the yellow notebook, I called the court records department in Hawaii, forgetting about the time difference. Hours. Years. I couldn't wait. I had to find Maryann. Judge Au had sentenced her to a minimum of ten years. She would be out. She must be out. She would be forty by now.

While I did the laundry I kept eyeing the clock. I walked to the store for groceries and took in the summer look of the street. All the small front gardens were blooming. I stopped to look at a neighbour's roses while I wondered what to say to Maryann. How to tell her that I was the cause of her long life in prison. I could say I broke speed limits, shoved the dog through the door, locked it again, ran back to the car. Explain that Michael had planned on coming in to watch the trial – the final proceedings – so we parked the car and then both of us ran up the courthouse steps and into the polished hall. I remember the feel of the courtroom door, its smooth surface, and the eyes in the opening crack. I remember the whispering mouth of the bailiff. "You are excused. You are five minutes late." Five minutes. My pulse was furious.

Michael and I sat down with the other spectators. What I felt was rage and shame. Judge Au made his entrance. Then Jan Futa was pulling herself to her feet, looking feverish. Her hair was tied with a white silk scarf as if she might be ready to wave it in surrender, but the gold pen was between her fingers, firmly in place. Robbery One! Burglary in the First Degree! Kidnapping! Here she stopped and stared at the jury. "Let me remind you that it is not necessary that each element be committed by the defendant alone," she said quietly. "And there is another charge involved," she said then, turning to point at Maryann. She let the word out slowly, as if we had never heard it before. *Murder.* Both syllables clear. I reached in my bag and pulled out the yellow notebook with the bright red spine. I could write openly now. But the words on the page were staggering and limp. Futa argued that Maryann had everything to gain by lying. "She had nothing to lose and everything to gain and for that reason I will submit to you that she did lie to you. William didn't have to say anything about the events in Hawaii. A year after those events, Detective Jimon You had no suspects. There is no reason for William to have fabricated these events."

William, she said, was virtually controlled by Maryann. "The testimony of William and Mr. Leach," Futa said, "is very close. I submit the reason for this is that it is true. Who doesn't remember what happened? Maryann Acker. Quite conveniently there are many things she doesn't remember because it's hard to fabricate things if there is no basis of truth. Mr. Leach testified that William Acker 'looked as scared as I felt.' Mr. Acker is high-strung, nervous, not calm and collected like his wife. What was she doing most of the time? Looking straight ahead. Why? Because she did not want Mr. Leach to see her."

I studied the jurors, especially the third alternate who had taken my seat. I thought of the *heiau* on the Big Island I had visited with my parents on their last trip. It's called the City of Refuge because in old Hawaii a person could run there when they were about to be taken for sacrifice.

When Stephen Hioki rose for his own summation, he told the jury that the defendant was presumed to be innocent even now. "Let me take you back to the time Mr. Acker was testifying," he said quickly, as if he might be about to recite the entire case. "I was asking him details – where Larry was standing, etc. If you recall, Mr. Acker got defensive, abrasive – began to assert himself through the microphone – became a wiseacre on the stand with little respect for it." He looked around the courtroom. "I had touched upon a nerve," he concluded indignantly, raising his voice by a note.

The case against Maryann Acker came down to two versions of a murder, and Hioki had tried to unravel only one of them. He had made William his adversary and never let us close to Maryann's story. In the time it took the rest of us to eat lunch, the jury found her guilty of kidnapping, robbery, unauthorized control of a vehicle, burglary, and murder in the first degree.

16

When it was finally morning in Honolulu, I spoke to three women at the Hawaii Department of Public Safety. One was in charge of interstate inmates, one was in charge of dual-jurisdiction inmates, and one referred me to the other two. None of them knew about Maryann.

Next, the Internet, where looking for her went like this:

Maryann Acker = must have

Murder = must have

Hawaii = must have

California = must have

The Must Haves were because there may be other Maryann Ackers in the world, but it is unlikely she or they will have committed murder and, if so, unlikely that she or they will have committed it in both Hawaii and

California. As I was typing, the computer underlined two words as wrong: *Acker* and *murder*.

"Such a long time ago," said a woman at the California Department of Corrections, which I called next. "But wait," she said, looking through her own computer files. Then she told me that Maryann was still in prison. She was an inmate at the California Institution for Women (CIW) in Chino, about an hour out of L.A. Eighteen years after the trial in Honolulu, and twenty-two years after the crimes, she was still locked up not far from the place she'd been arrested in 1978.

June 28, 2000

Dear Maryann,
I was on your jury in Hawaii, but I was dismissed. I've been reading a notebook I kept during your trial and I'm wondering how you are doing.
Very sincerely,
Linda Spalding

I wrote the letter at our cottage in the country, where I was alone for three days. I had no car, no way to get out except by walking a mile to the highway and then maybe hitching a ride. There was nobody within shouting or even screaming distance. And I'd been waking up in the middle of the night with the familiar clutch – a feeling that everything was slipping away. Why imagine that a woman in prison for twenty-two years would read my letter with any interest in writing back? How, if she did answer, would I explain the part I had played in her life? If I had been there that morning, been there on time, you'd be free. Up there in the country the river sounds like an engine left running, like a buzz of static that is constant, rattling, each crash crashing into the next crash before the last one has finished. There are no commas, no apostrophes. Out beyond trees, spirits wander. The river was thrumming and I called my mother, who would soon be among the spirits. I called her in order to hear a human voice. She had been out to dinner with her friend. "She does so much for me," my mother confessed. "It makes me feel dependent."

I said it was good for both of them; it works both ways.

"How's that? What can I ever do for her?"

"You provide the comfort of need."

"She has family."

"It's not the same." I said this although, lately, I hung on my mother's words as to a lifeline. I should have recorded her, but I knew I would never replay our conversations after she died. I actually have a record of my brother's voice, but it would kill me to hear it. The dead are with me all the time. Day in. Day out. Only I miss the flesh.

I grieved for my mother even as I talked to her, and little by little I gave her more of myself. "I think I have arthritis in my knee," I said that night, trusting her with this small fear for the first time.

"It's not so bad," she said. "I had it in my hands and it went away. It comes. It goes. Don't worry too much about it." Sensible and consoling words, which meant I still had a mother, thank God.

"I remember when you stopped knitting."

"Yes."

"And did it really hurt?"

"Yes. But I did something. Heat, probably, because I like heat. And anyway it stopped. It doesn't bother me now."

"But it makes me feel old."

"Well you aren't."

What does old mean, I wondered, to a woman who buried her husband when he was fifty-nine, her son at fifty-seven, and she's almost ninety? One day a few years ago, but after my brother had died in his plane, she went to the doctor for a checkup. I was visiting, sitting at the table when she came home and burst into tears. (I've seen her cry only three times.) "I'm absolutely fine. There's nothing wrong with me!" Her collapsed face, her collapsed expression. Shame. Horror. To have survived.

17

July 16, 2000

Dear Linda,

I received your card today, and to say I was totally overwhelmed is the understatement of the year! You, of course, have no idea what's been going on recently to cause my astonishment. I just found out last night that a Writ of *Habeas Corpus* on the Hawaii case was filed last week. Then, I got your card. Today! The timing is really incredible in my opinion. I have a feeling you might have made a difference! Were you an alternate juror? Is that why you were dismissed? There are so many things I would like to ask you, but I do want to thank you, from my heart, for writing to me.

A few months after my original sentence in Hawaii, the Paroling Authority reset my minimum term. They increased it to 30 years. That's why this writ is so important to me. I have been incarcerated for 22 years now. I was so ~~insane~~ naïve then, but feeling like I knew all there was to know and that I could handle the world. When we arrived in Hawaii he really turned my world upside down. In my trial, I testified very truthfully. I was terrified of William and in fear for my life. Today, I see so many things I could have done. But I guess that's the big difference between being 18 and 40. I have grown so much, and learned so much about myself. Again, I sincerely thank you! I hope I will hear from you again, and please, feel free to ask me any questions you may have.

Sincerely,
Maryann

It was August by the time I got this letter in Toronto, and I carried it back up to the cottage along with shorts and jeans and the yellow notebook. Driving east, I looked out at the summer countryside along the 401, where the corn was ripening under a silky sky. I'd moved to Canada when I was thirty-nine, coming to a place where I had no friends, no network of support, and where things with my newly constituted family were electric and complex. Overnight my children had shed their Hawaii childhoods like embarrassing skins, and within six months I hardly knew them or myself. I had been burning bridges forever but, as I looked out at Lake Ontario, stretched like a wall between my two countries, I saw Maryann as a link to my former life.

Thirty years. The average sentence for a felony in Hawaii is four or five. Even syndicate killers don't get more than twenty. That night I dreamed about her prison bed. It was iron, painted dark green. On it a coloured quilt, very bright, made by someone in her family, blues and red against stark white cotton. In the dream, I admired her for possessing such a quilt, and yet I was surprised, as if I assumed we could not have the same taste. Someone in her family had made it and she kept it in her otherwise undecorated cell. The quilt was a proclamation. The dream was about Maryann as part of a family, as part of my American past. When I woke up, I lay in bed drinking a cup of coffee and staring out at the rain, trying to remember if there had ever been a day when I woke with sufficient joy. All that came to mind were the few days of my childhood when my brother was home from college, mornings with an ecstatic murmur that wouldn't be stilled, like romantic love without a premonition of sadness. Otherwise I look back on mornings when I loved getting up to my girls. They were tousled, beautiful, getting ready for a dance class or birthday party.

Then I thought of my grandmother's Kansas City house, which I visited for a two-week period every summer of my childhood. I thought of the lovely solitude of those lost summer days although they consist, now, in a series of images much like a dream that, when told, dissolves immediately. I suppose there was the liberation from my parents to take into account, although in all other ways the brief interlude with my grandmother was more con-strained than the rest of my life. I should explain that my grandmother was deaf, that we learned, over the years, to move through our days and evenings in silent harmony, that she worked happily in her sewing room while I was left to my fantasies.

One summer it was hotter than the ordinary hundred-plus degrees and we created a space in her unfinished basement where we spent all our waking hours. Without her sewing machine, my grandmother embroidered or crocheted. I was embroidering something myself – a flannelette baby smock – but I painted pictures too, and wrote stories. I filled the pages of my diary. It was harder to live in my imagination down there, with my watchful grandmother so close, but she was a woman who had lived alone for so many years that she considered it no affront to sit in silent companionship. The smock was for my brother's first child, who was yet to be born and whose short life was to be my first tragedy. But that summer, as long as I didn't move from my wicker chair, I was safe.

Under a window of the country house, I had been making a garden – a vanity among all the pine trees and birches, all the grass and stone and water. Children grown and the decisive acts of my life behind me, I had been trying to believe I was in the summer of my life. The garden, small as it was, had been a laying of claim and a slight breaking of the stern rules we adopted on taking over the land. Only to perch, not to civilize. When we first came up here it was just a year after Maryann's trial and this house, with its broken deck and pointy roof and stilts, was as precarious as we felt.

18

Her letters were handwritten. "You say that you are oddly connected to my story. Do you remember the circumstances of why you were replaced on the jury?" When I received mail from Maryann, I read the lines and then I read between the lines because the words were so perfectly formed and spelled and punctuated. "I was so young when I got arrested. I had only been out on my own for a few months before my fateful meeting with William. There is so much I've never experienced. In some ways I feel that, emotionally, I'm still stuck at 18." Yes. Her letters reminded me of the girl I was when I met Philip.

"I would have done the same thing if it came to a sick animal," Maryann wrote when I finally told her why I'd been thrown off her jury. "But darn that vet for at least not keeping him til the end of the day! All of that, however, is water under the bridge. One thing I have learned over the years is to learn from the past but not to dwell on all the 'what ifs.' That doesn't really serve any constructive purpose."

Constructive purpose? I sent a postcard that said: "I can't remember what was wrong with the dog. It must have been more or less serious . . . but really! It wasn't worth thirty years of your life."

I was interested in that prison life but what I wanted to hear about was her life before. I wanted to dwell on all the what-ifs. What the poet Tomas Tranströmer calls a book that can only be read in the dark. I asked her if she could describe the house where she grew up, but she told me about the jobs she had held at CIW. She told me about the degree she had earned and her hobbies and the organizations she belonged to. She said she had served her full sentence in California, but they were still holding her because of Hawaii. "If Hawaii grants the Writ of *Habeas Corpus*, the prosecutor will have to decide whether to re-try me. If not, my commitment on the other Hawaii charges will be completed in October, 2001."

Since the trial, Maryann had been out of her prison only once, when she was driven into L.A. for a dental appointment. By then, she was nervous about going out. She was nervous about being shackled. She was nervous about seeing a strange dentist. In the van, she peered through small, barred windows to look at cars, shops, and houses. What she saw was the freeway, a long slice of the present tense.

Late that summer, I drove back to Toronto in order to do something I had delayed, along with my guilt about Maryann, for eighteen years. I'd been living in a country I had no claim to, dividing my time between a house in downtown Toronto and one that stretches between a dirt road and a river. But finally, I had applied for Canadian citizenship. All my life, I had excused myself from membership. I had lived without affiliation or ceremony. Even my wedding to Philip was an elopement. But now, I wanted something more, unlike Maryann, who would emerge from prison without attachment to anything.

Sitting across from me in the waiting room at the Department of Immigration was a young woman nursing a baby, breasts full of promise. I watched her. I was the only American in the room. After a time, when we had to line up and show ourselves with a picture ID, a Muslim woman was taken to a corner, where her veil was lifted while official eyes flicked over her and checked her photograph. Two men who had come with her glared and clenched their fists. Finally we were ushered into the room where we were to make an oath of allegiance to the Queen.

The doors were locked behind us. A skinny clerk in a black robe went through an hour of instructions – when to stand up, sit down. This was followed by thirty brief minutes of ceremony during which a tape deck punched out "O Canada!," though not without static. There were small conversations among those of us who were alternately sitting and standing: Where were you born? How long here? Could you take my picture, please, when I go up? If it is possible to be moved by the sight of a tape deck on a table, I was, though a glance at the photo of a young Queen Elizabeth made me, momentarily, wish to bolt. What would my father think of my desire to be taken in by Loyalists?

I had called my mother, having told her nothing through the process of application but suddenly wanting her to understand what I was doing as if, like a secret marriage, it would otherwise be null and void. She said it was wonderful to become a citizen of Canada, where I lived, and that I had lost nothing and gained something I valued. It was not the response I had expected, but in losing her short-term memory, most of her long-term friends, and her husband and son, she had lost her bitterness and become the mother of my dreams.

Back at the cottage, my big orange lilies were nodding by the east wall of the house. The yellow daisies were bowing. The delphiniums were blue to a fault and petunias pushed against the rocks. It was this, exactly, that I wanted to be: fully in bloom, evident and engaged. I wanted to belong here, where I had sprinkled the ashes of my brother and his wife, where we had buried our cat and dog, where we measure our lives. The stretch of house is at right angles to the water, so that only the end where we sleep has any view of it. And the river itself makes a right-angle turn in front of us, rushing down a set of rapids, pouring over rocks and pieces of the Shield that make portaging so difficult and walking such joy.

19

Maryann grew up in Phoenix, where her family was closely connected to the church. They were devout. Believers. These are the facts I was given over the next few months. It all sounded regular. Her sister, Penne, was nine years older. Everything, in fact, had already happened to this family long before Maryann was born: two brothers had died, one as an infant, one at the age of fourteen. But when I asked Maryann about her childhood, I got happy snapshots: learning to whistle when she was six months old, when she was two, getting a rocking chair. "I was born accident-prone. There's a picture of me sitting in that rocking chair with a black eye." At three, it was a tricycle, which she rode into her sister's room one Christmas morning before anyone else was up.

There is also this: until she was four, only two men were allowed to carry her. When anyone else tried, she'd scream.

Her mother was a housewife, although she once worked as a cashier in the *Phoenix Gazette* building. "I was still young, so I'm not sure why she went to work. Whether she just wanted to or if it was financially necessary." Whatever the reason, Gladys Bray didn't work for long. She went back to baking, washing, tending her family, and serving the church community like an acolyte.

Bert was the easygoing parent. Quick to laugh, he seemed to like everyone and kept his job as a salesman for McKesson & Robbins for thirty years. Born a Baptist in Texas, he converted to Mormonism when the first baby died.

Death. Maryann gave me the facts as if she had given them a hundred times. The baby had swallowed a paper clip. The other son had died of an asthma attack. I could imagine Gladys with baby Maryann, jealously guarding her every step. I could imagine her shaking her head, saying no and no and no, making too many rules for a child of Maryann's temperament. Because, according to the Mormon Church – or the Church of Jesus Christ of Latter-day Saints – rules are the most important part of life. All this because Joseph Smith discovered twelve gold tablets in a cave under a hill in New York State. Young Joseph had been told about the tablets by an angel named

Moroni, and he deciphered them by reading through a peep stone in a hat. The book that resulted – The Book of Mormon – is said to be as divine as the New Testament. "Obedience is the first law of heaven," preaches this church. Obedience to the law of the church rather than the law of the state. Obedience as explained by living prophets. I know about this because of that great-grandmother who joined the Saints when one of her children died. The story is that they promised to reunite the family after death and in a fervour of hope, she moved the family out of Brown County, Kansas, where they owned thousands of acres of the richest wheat land in the world, to Independence, Missouri, where the early Saints had built their version of Zion. The move defined my future, but that is the story of the world.

Mormons are taught that life is a test, that they have been plucked out of heaven and brought to earth to try on the temptation of free will. In Maryann's household, the tests were challenging. By the time Maryann was nine, Penne had fallen in love with a black man, become pregnant, broken her church's covenant and her mother's heart. Only Maryann was left to compensate for the family failings while Gladys's relatives refused to speak to any of them. Gladys and her children were shunned. "It was hard hard on my mom. Her own father was terrible to us. Her whole family was. After that we never saw much of them."

But the religion of prophets and rules continued to be an integral part of daily life. There were lessons before school. There were the Monday evenings when all Mormon families read from The Book of Mormon. There were the other six days of the week, each of them regulated by sanctions and doctrine. Tuesday nights were for Mutual meetings. Other nights were given over to Beehive Girls or Gleaner Girls. There was Sunday school and the Young Adult Group.

My own family was ashamed of the Saints, although they went along to Independence, burning bridges all the way. My father was that mad, grief-stricken woman's grandson, raised to be obedient but also to think. Critical Thinking was the core of his faith. The training in thinking came from his father, who had watched his family disintegrate. It came from his mother, who was a teacher. It came from law school. It was something he taught me. Never believe in prophets, false or otherwise. Always question. Question everything.

20

As our letters became more frequent, I tried to make mine more personal so that Maryann would do the same. I told her about eloping and running away to Mexico. I told her that Philip had left college and me, and that finding him in Mazatlan five months later felt like a miracle. I'd called an operator in Mexico City and she had tried every beach town and village, finally locating him in a bar, where he had been sleeping on a table.

"I miss you."

"So come on down."

"You know I can't do that. My parents would freak. I can't travel with you unless we get married."

I told Maryann that an hour later Philip called again and I drove from Boulder to Tucson in the backseat of our best friend's father's car. Listening to the radio. Had a white cotton suit in a white suitcase. My hair up in curlers.

Maryann wrote back saying her parents had moved her from Phoenix to Yuma when she was fourteen and that marked the end of her childhood. "Mom and I argued a lot and I stayed gone a lot. Dad would come home and have to play peacemaker. By the way, did I mention I was a daddy's girl?"

She had left a good friend in Phoenix, a girl she had met in the sixth grade named Mariann. Now, at the tender age of fourteen, she began to slip away on weekends, taking a bus back to Phoenix to stay with her friend. Attached like Kahlo's painting of the two Fredas, they were both slender, with long, brown hair. The other Mariann was serious about church and God and being good, but when they went to the mall to skate, Maryann showed her how to flirt, how to drink and smoke, things she was learning in Yuma. I read this with some surprise. Hadn't she said, in court, that William had introduced her to alcohol and cigarettes? It was there in my yellow notebook. By sixteen, she had a driver's licence and drove herself back and forth between Yuma and Phoenix, three hundred miles each way. She swore to herself that she would go back to Phoenix for good as soon as she was done with high school. "Which is exactly what I did," she wrote. "Which is how I met William."

The letters were taking us someplace, but I was asking myself all over again whether, given the drive out to Hanauma Bay, she might not have pulled the gun on William. (Stop! Thief! Get out of this car. Joe and I would prefer to go back to the bar and dance!) I was asking myself whether she might not have run out onto a sidewalk in the afternoon sunshine and shouted for help. Maybe it was because my mind was not made up in 1982 that I had made myself late on that last day. Maybe I wanted a second chance.

Dear Linda,
I didn't consciously think about it at the time, but on some level I knew mom & dad would hate William, which made him all the more attractive. I 'needed' to be loved and accepted, to have someone else validate my existence and my worth. As long as I agreed with him, he fulfilled that need. Think Charles Manson and you'll have a good picture of the type of personality William has. I honestly believe, had he been free longer during his life, he would have had a 'following'. He was a very charismatic, manipulative man. From the time he was 14 until today, and he's 51 now, he's only been free for 14 months of his life. (This little tidbit I found out about after I was arrested.) But in that fourteen months he managed to collect two wives!

Today I read his Board Transcripts and realize what an ass he makes of himself; how absurd much of what he says sounds. But back then . . .

Two wives?

With the letter, she enclosed an article from *California Legal Magazine*. Its title is "Where Is William Acker?" and it says William is five feet eleven inches tall and weighs one hundred and sixty-five pounds. It says he's been in trouble with the law since he was six, but that his record is closed because he's in the prison witness protection program. Moved from one prison to another, from one state to another, he's provided information in a dozen cases, including one against Jesse Gonzales, who is now on death row because of William's testimony. Making deals with prosecutors around the country, but especially in L.A., he has created an interesting life for himself. And it all began in 1978, when Bert Bray called the sheriff's office in Yuma.

William says he testifies against fellow prisoners in order to bring moral balance to his life. At parole hearings he maintains that, although he participated in the robberies immediately preceding the murders of Larry Hasker and Cesario Arauza, his wife shot the victims. In 1991, however, he told the parole board something different.

21

Parole Hearing, William Acker, 1991

. . .

COMMISSIONER O'CONNELL: Okay. What have you discussed in therapy?

INMATE ACKER: Well, just about the criminal personality seminar. Basically that criminals want to blame everyone else for their criminal activity. I've done that myself, you know . . .

COMM. O'CONNELL: Well, tell me how you've done that then.

INMATE ACKER: How have I done that?

COMM. O'CONNELL: Right. How have you changed?

INMATE ACKER: Well, I don't make victims of people no more.

COMM. O'CONNELL: Okay, then answer me this: Did you commit the murder for which you're in custody?

INMATE ACKER: Yes, I did.

COMM. O'CONNELL: What about the one in Hawaii?

INMATE ACKER: I committed them all and I want the woman behind it, the woman that's incarcerated, I would like her set free.

COMM. O'CONNELL: Okay. So Marianne [phonetic] didn't do anything?

INMATE ACKER: Absolutely nothing.

COMM. O'CONNELL: And is this the first time you've said that?

INMATE ACKER: The very first time.

COMM. O'CONNELL: Okay. And this is a change of attitude because of this class you took?

INMATE ACKER: Listen to me. Marianne Bray [phonetic] has a good family, a family that's willing to help her. Okay?

COMM. O'CONNELL: Yes.

INMATE ACKER: She's always had that.

COMM. O'CONNELL: Yes.

INMATE ACKER: Give her that chance.

COMM. O'CONNELL: Yes, I'm aware of that. It is difficult, however, to give somebody a parole date when she's sitting there looking at two counts of murder. One of them based solely upon your testimony in

Hawaii and the other one, again, based upon your testimony in California.

INMATE ACKER: Well the DA's office last board hearing made a real strong point of what I did, you know. In other words, he didn't accept my testimony. So let him stand by that decision. Let him make that decision. Let him make – let that office stand by what they write, what they do, and free that woman. She deserves to be free.

When Maryann read the magazine article in 1992, she sent it to the University of Southern California Wrongful Conviction Project. Would the article help her get paroled?

One of the law students telephoned Stephen Hioki, wondering if there were any records of the trial. Hioki told the student that Hawaii routinely destroyed court transcripts ten years after a trial, but that there was something they should know about Maryann's sentencing. Judge Au had used the word *accomplice* in his instructions to the jury. And this was improper, Hioki said, because Maryann hadn't been tried as an accomplice; she'd been tried as the shooter. "At least one jury member said he didn't think she pulled the trigger," Hioki remembered. "So they must have thought the judge gave them permission to find her guilty even if she didn't do it." Hioki said that he had petitioned the court for a judgment of acquittal or a new

trial only a month after Maryann was sentenced based on
Judge Au's improper instructions. He said the petition was
denied. Then he said that a plea of *habeas corpus* might be
worth trying.

22

That fall, Michael and I were going to spend three months in New York. "Have a safe trip," Maryann wrote. "New York seems like an exciting, yet intimidating city, although I've never been there."

I promised to tell her everything. Seeing things for someone else would be like motherhood all over again. The pleasure of being a conduit. For Maryann, I went to the public library and looked at the vaulted ceilings, marble floors, and rooms that contain the secrets of existence. I went to the Tenement Museum, and the Pierpont Morgan Library, where I saw an exhibit of John Ruskin drawings, manuscripts, and letters. I told Maryann that the Tenement Museum had the kind of apartments that our ancestors probably lived in when they crossed the

Atlantic from Europe. I said the Ruskin exhibit cost $5 to enter and that his work is autobiographical and that he was an only child whose mother was intensely religious. All through his childhood, I said, she made him memorize sections of the Bible. He was expected to enter the ministry, but instead, he had a breakdown. I said maybe that was what had happened to her and, as I wrote, I imagined Maryann's mother looming over her with The Book of Mormon in hand, telling her to believe it or else.

I told her that up in Times Square a man was living in a block of ice.

In her next letter, Maryann said she knew all about breakdowns. She said during her first years in prison, she had come very close. "I spent many weekends my first couple of years here getting drunk on homemade wine. Most of it's pretty nasty-tasting stuff. But, once you get the first glassful down, you really don't taste the rest."

I kept writing. I told Maryann about the groceries I was buying and how much they cost and what I did with them when I got them home to my rented kitchen. I told her about the movies I was seeing and about an exhibit of photographs taken in the nineteenth century when Ruskin was writing his books and falling in love with a ten-year-old child named Rose la Touche. The photographs were portraits of an Italian contessa who asked the photographer to lengthen her neck and reduce her waist.

Maryann wrote back: "Sometimes I imagine the kind of place I could afford and where I would choose to live and how I would spend my time. I think about the very reduced social life I would have if I got out of here and then about how it would be entirely my own. I mean my life. We women are so new at forging our own identities."

I had no interest in forging a new identity. I was stuck on the past. I told Maryann that it was hard to know whether the Countess Castiglione had created herself or disguised herself in those photographs. I said that if I were locked up the way she was I'd probably spend all my time trying to recreate my childhood. I'd remember the feel of the carpet on the stairs, I'd remember the smell of the kitchen sink or the dustiness of potatoes in the white metal bin in the dark pantry, where things rarely used were kept. I told her that my brother was once in the hospital, unable to speak or move, and he kept himself sane by recalling our grandparents' house – every inch of it! He began in a corner of the kitchen and made himself remember pictures on the walls, doorknobs, floor surfaces, ceilings, cracks, nails, placement of furniture, salt shakers, dishes, curtains, sounds, smells.

I told her that if I could steal my own life and put it in a glass-topped box, I'd probably do it, then hold it in my hand, run a finger around it. Not because the contents are beautiful, but because they are contained, visible, embalmed. Open the box and pick around at the pieces. I said I wished she would do that for me, starting with the house where she lived when she was a child. "A simple description," I said.

I told her the man who encased himself in ice had reemerged. "Must go to sleep," were his first words. "Can't talk. Can't think."

23

Dear Linda,

My little cell is 8 x 10. As you walk in the door, which has a little window in the middle for the staff to see in, the bunk bed is straight ahead. To the right of the door are two metal lockers and a metal desk with a stool on the left that swings out. To the left of the door is the sink and on the wall around the corner from the sink is the toilet, facing the bunks. Valere – my cell mate – drew a diagram of the room, which I'll enclose. On the wall between the toilet and the bunk are two metal shelves. The bunks, of course, are metal also. Years ago the institution provided wooden lock boxes that we could utilize for storage and they fit perfectly at the foot of the bed. The lid flips all the way back, the opening is toward the mattress, so now it's a shelf and storage, and a good place to write. We are also allowed footlockers, at least for the time being. Valere and I each have one. My tiny TV sits on one. In the past we were allowed to receive personal blankets, sheets, towels, rugs and I've managed to hang on to some things and it helps give the room a better feel. Even though the blanket and bedspread are worn and old, it still helps. I have a latch-hook rug of a wolf on the floor. They are leaning toward making us get rid of all our little comforts which really used to upset and depress me. Now, I just wish they would do what they are going to do and quit messing with us and threatening us. I do like having these little touches of "home", but for a little while longer, I can do without them until I get out and really have a place of my own to call home!

I'm on the top bunk, so I can get up here and kind of be in my own little world. During my lunch breaks during the week, I have the room to myself. It's limited and I'm never just totally by myself, but in my mind I can take myself far away from here. One of my dreams is to, one day, be able to travel. I would love to see Europe like that contessa.

Love ya,
Maryann

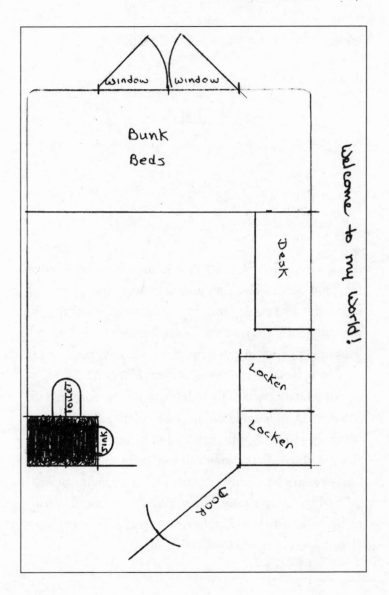

24

In January, Michael and I flew home after a snowstorm that smothered New York and then New Year's Eve with thousands of people jamming the streets, watching the year 2000 tick away on the Times Square clock. The millennium, when things were supposed to change.

There were no more letters from Maryann.

By March it was still colder than hell in Toronto (I'm convinced hell is cold) and brutally colourless. This is our famous dog-shit month, when all of it rises to the surface, along with used condoms and the inorganic crap of city life – plastic bags, coffee cups, frozen cigarette butts. I kept telling people about finding Maryann, about writing to her. I found myself referring to her as my prisoner. "Don't you care if she's guilty?" people asked.

I said I was trying to find out if I cared.

Still no letters.

We were going to be in California for two weeks. Near Corona. Near the prison. I wrote to ask if I could visit her, telling myself that my interest was rational. Maybe I'd made myself late on that last day. Maybe not. Maybe I was trying to find out how much I owed her.

When the last ice disappears and a bit of green emerges, Toronto becomes feverish: deck chairs dragged out of basements, hoses attached to spigots, gardens raked, windows washed. In May, one is glad to have experienced the confinement of winter. Touching the ground, breathing the outside air is bliss. I told myself that the next part of Maryann's life might be like this. She would be sent to Hawaii for the hearing. In my head, I created a vision of her wearing the soft blue muumuu. I saw her unchained, walking through the courthouse, going out through the huge double doors. From the top of the steps she would look up at the volcanic mountains and beautiful Punchbowl, the extinct volcano under which she once lived. She would adjust her shoulders, unflex her fists. Finally the clock face would crack. Time would begin.

25

I am standing outside a confessional. It's a novelty to me, but apparently I would like to be invited in. I am standing on one foot and then the other, waiting. Go on in! It's time to confess!

But I'm not Catholic!

Never mind about that! The priest will listen to you regardless.

It occurs to me that, in spite of my sins (acts for which I crave forgiveness), what I want to tell the priest is that I've lost my faith. I no longer believe in anything. Perhaps he can offer some advice? I must say, it's odd to dream so directly from life since I have, indeed, felt a sudden draining away of the mystical belief that usually sustains me. There have been times when the sustenance was thin, when I was full of shame and despair. But the shame meant that the faith was still there, lurking. This is different.

I write to Maryann about this dream. I ask her about faith. Does she still have it? Did it leave her and then return, like a lost pet? What about my idea of visiting her?

Maryann sends back an application for visiting privileges. With it is a list describing the rules for the prison visiting room. It says that prisoners are allowed one bracelet, one necklace with charm or religious medallion, one pair of stud earrings, one watch, and two rings. They may not bring in bags or eyeglass cases or cigarette cases or Bibles. They must wear bras and underpants and they may not use the restroom during a visit.

No drinking cups, ink pens, or umbrellas are allowed. Also no kissing or touching. Embracing may occur when a visitor enters and leaves. No sitting on laps, except for small children. No sitting on the tops of tables or sitting straddled on the bench. No sitting between the legs of visitors.

No mention of faith.

26

The only prisons I have seen are in movies.

This one looks like a big, brick, sprawling elementary school. Built for eight hundred women, it holds twice that many and is surrounded by a twenty-foot-high double chain-link steel fence. On top of the fence is a big roll of barbed wire. And around all of this are dairy farms on a scale that is hard to believe. Thousands of dairy cows waiting to be milked, their necks between steel bars.

The waiting room. All those children. Babies in the arms of young fathers. Babies in the arms of grandmothers waiting to visit mothers. And children waiting to visit grandmothers. A family of nine waiting for three hours on the plastic chairs all in a row, the father commanding obedience, not to move, not to wiggle, not to turn and look into the visiting room where the grandmother would become visible.

It makes me feel faint.

There are no magazines to read. No pictures at which to look. "Do you want me to take you out to the van?" the menacing father asks. "Right now? Do you know what that means?" The old fear hits me and I try to make friends with the children to compensate, to make their daddy see that they are innocents. I picture Maryann as she waits for her call. I picture her trying to remember the other side of the steel fence.

There is, first, an outside waiting area. Then the inside waiting room. In the outside area there are flies. They cover feet and faces and hands as visitors sit in the shade of the cement-block shelter fanning themselves. But inside we are grim, having passed, one by one, through the metal detector, having put the items we are carrying into a tray and having passed through the electronic gate. We are carrying only a car key, thirty one-dollar bills, and a driver's licence in a clear plastic bag. "When's Gramma coming?" The line of children try to peer through the smudgy glass as their father enforces straight backs and parallel knees. "Do you want to go out to the van?" The baby is thirsty and cries for two hours. There is nothing to drink.

For two hours we suffer a misery that is a form of penance or a punishment for coming to visit those who are here to be punished. As each prisoner is led into the visiting room, she can be viewed through the dirty glass. Making her way through prisoners and visitors who are shouting and hugging and holding each other, she stops at a line drawn on the floor and waits for the door to be buzzed open, for her mother or sister or husband to cross the line.

I have that picture in my mind of the fragile girl behind big glasses, her soft blond hair, her steady walk, and when I see her cross the crowded room, I know her immediately. She moves as if she is off somewhere else. There is that calm, as if all the important questions have already been asked. Then the door is buzzed open and her arms are around me. "It's so good to actually see you." Her hug is fierce.

I am fumbling at my wad of one-dollar bills. No one comes to visit without buying food for the inmate; this much, during the long wait and the observation through glass, has become clear. No inmate comes into the visiting area without being summoned by a visitor and no inmate leaves the visiting area with anything at all – no gift, no souvenir, not even a grain of popcorn. We must consume whatever we buy on the spot. Burritos can be pulled from a machine, carried to the microwave oven and heated.

There are hot drinks, cold drinks, snacks, and ice-cream bars, even fresh fruit. The selection is fantastic.

Maryann is pointing to the buttons, the slot for bills, the place for coins. The prisoners are not allowed to handle money. "Let's go find a seat." Like everyone else – all the prisoners – she's wearing jeans, sneakers, a grey T-shirt. Her hair is short and her rimless glasses are slightly tinted, the kind that darken in sunlight. While I fumble at the slot for change, she retrieves the food and then leads me out to the cement tables in the open air. We pass the children and their grandmother, who has a warm and intelligent face. "That's Beth. And her best friend. The family always fills out forms for both of them because Gena doesn't get other visitors. It gives her a chance to see someone." Eleven of them around the table, with various board games unfurled along with cards. Beth and Gena, she says, killed husbands. Most of the lifers are here for that. In this way, she is different. At another table a little boy's mother and grandmother watch as he runs on the grass. He has spent three hours waiting to get to his mother. Before that, the ride in a hot car, the slicking back of hair, the starchy shirt, while now his mother is distracted. Her eyes are elsewhere.

"It's nothing like prisons in movies, is it?"

I say, "So many older women. Grandmothers. And I can't get over how ordinary everyone looks."

"Any one of us could be your neighbour, right?" Maryann pauses. Then she says, "And you could just as easily be in here."

I stretch out my legs. For several days I've been worried about this one-on-one conversation with someone I've never met. I've been imagining the awkwardness of wanting to get up and leave. Of being bored. Of running out of talk. Now, the first thing I want to say is that I'm stunned by the ugliness of this place; would it be so hard to have a few plants, a few colours, something for the kids besides one set of swings? But that wouldn't be polite. Even if she didn't choose the décor, this is where she has to live. It represents all she has of a public face.

At times like this people try to establish things they have in common, but all we have is a few days in a Honolulu courtroom and the fact that we both got married in Arizona, that I know how it feels to be out on a limb, sawing it off. I could say I recognized some kind of kinship that first day in court, but how much would I be embroidering? I could talk about a night in Guadalajara when Philip's friend, Roberto, pulled a gun on a stranger who asked me to dance. I was twenty years old and it was thrilling.

The California Institution for Women is run by the state. Maryann says it was built to look like a campus back in the 1950s, when the brick housing units were called cottages and each woman had a cell to herself. But when Ronald Reagan became governor of California, the cells got double- and triple-bunked. Beds were put in the auditorium and the gym. Programs were cut. Now, lifers are told that any trouble will get them shipped north. To a tougher place. "The new prisons are so much worse." While Maryann explains this, she's giving me time to get my bearings. We have our food spread out on our laps, and she's saying that CIW has two kinds of inmates. The drug user is Level 2. Maryann and the other lifers are Level 4. "And allowed a little more leeway." But no conjugal visits. "The men ruined that for us."

"How so?"

"Well, their women got pregnant, then had to go on welfare."

"So this is the only kind of visit allowed."

"But in the old days we could have a whole weekend in a special house. With our family or husband. But not now."

"Your folks used to come?"

She nods. "Every chance they got. And when they couldn't drive, a few times my sister brought them. Then my mom died from cancer four years ago and after that Dad didn't give a rip any more. I lost him this past July, the day before his eighty-fourth birthday."

"Are you and your sister close?"

"She won't take my calls. They run up her phone bill. When I was adopted, she just never got over it."

"You were adopted?"

"I never told you?"

At last I am on to something. It is an afternoon in the winter of 1961 and a clerk at the county courthouse in Phoenix decides not to take her lunch break. Everyone else has left the building, but she wants to catch up on the work that's been piling up. She's rummaging through a stack of papers next to the phone when a man comes through the door, panting, out of breath. He's come up the stairs at a run. He wipes his hands on his trousers. "Where do I adopt a baby?" he blurts out.

"You want a baby?"

"No, ma'am. I already have one. Or rather my son does. Or rather my stepson. Does."

The clerk studies the man. He's young, in his early forties, and he's wearing the clothes of a working man. "Where is this baby?" she asks softly, so as not to frighten him, and meanwhile she reaches across the pile of papers and edges the heavy telephone closer to her chair. She has not stood up or changed the look on her face, which is calm and businesslike.

"At its mother's . . ." He shakes his head. "But that's no problem, ma'am, believe you me."

The clerk has the number in her head. "Just a sec. Maybe I can help." Her friend Gladys. And Bert. Lost their boy just two months ago to an asthma attack. She feels no need to explain herself. All her work at the court-house, all her work for the church, all her life has taught her to think of the greater need. No reason to explain that their first baby died and now they've lost the boy . . . it's nobody's business and anyway the phone is ringing. "Gladys! Get Bert quick. I have a baby for you!" The clerk covers the receiver with her hand and whispers, "I forgot to ask. Girl or boy?" Then, taking her hand away, shouts, "No kidding! I mean it. Get Bert right over here this minute." Now Maryann looks at me. "That's the way it begins," she says, "my story. In a courthouse."

We sit there for a long, long minute.

"Were they overly protective, your parents?"

"I was cherished."

"Except for your sister."

"Well, she was attached to her brother who died." She looks away, defensive. "Do you have a sister?"

I say no. I say my brother died ten years ago. Crashed his plane and killed himself and his second wife. I say my father died the same summer my husband walked out and for a minute I can see the tail of something disappear just around the corner of my mind. I want to call it back, but

Maryann is saying that her parents just wanted her to marry a good person and have a good life. "That's all. Mom actually loved my first boyfriend."

"The one before William?"

"I mentioned Doug in a letter. Remember? Returned missionary. Six two. Sandy hair. Good-looking. He was the reason I moved back to Phoenix. Well, which I wanted to do anyway, I guess. But just think. If I'd adhered to the teachings of chastity, morality, and faithfulness . . . who knows? But I met William during Doug's business trip. Met him and married him before Doug even came back. Like that" – snapping her fingers – "I really wasn't thinking seriously of getting married at eighteen. I still wanted to live my life." She stops talking and listens, as if there is another conversation going on in her head. Then she says, "I wanted to make everybody happy." Another silence. "Be a rebel and a pleaser. I was running around behind their backs giving my parents the blues before I hit sixteen. Then I moved back to Phoenix. So I didn't have to sneak around after that."

The landlady had a sofa. Maryann had brought her waterbed from home and she built a new frame for it. She got dressed in the morning and went to work at Arizona Hardware, the same distribution company that employed her father. At work, she was pleasant to people and when a co-worker mentioned a brother who was coming to stay, Maryann showed polite interest. "She said he'd had a rough life. She said he was a sweet guy who needed some-one to care about him."

Doug was away on that business trip.

And William got a job working for Arizona Hardware in the warehouse. One day he came inside and met Maryann. It was after lunch, sometime in the afternoon. He was sweating a little. He had the look of something abandoned, like the kitten she had taken in a few weeks before. He had a mother in California. And the sister. But he was just out of jail and he talked a blue streak. "At eight-een I wasn't thinking about who this guy is. . . ." They went out the evening of the day they met and then he came back to her place as if he belonged to her. It was the lost cat all over again. He needed her. It was a new experience and it excited her. There had always been expectations, always, but never like this. The way he came straight at her. He didn't know any better than that. He wasn't expe-rienced. It was what she thought about. Helping him. The way he reached out to touch her to prove something to himself. The way his future was up to her. He liked to drink, unlike Doug, but for Maryann it was a daytime nighttime shift, two sides of herself, light and dark. "Bill was so exciting to be with. It wasn't like anything I'd ever experienced ever, being with him."

She had that kitten, eight weeks old, who refused to be in the same room with him. Whenever he came home, the kitten hid, ran to a closet or under the bed. "I should have paid attention. The kitten was right. Once, it jumped down from the window over the bed and bit him hard. He had taken a shower and was lying there naked. He screamed. That kitten bit him in the balls," Maryann told me. She grinned.

Within days of moving in, William was talking marriage. "He kept bugging me about it and then he caught me one day when I just said, Yeah, okay, just to shut him up. But the next thing I knew, I was calling my parents."

While she's telling me this, I remember William on the witness stand saying, "We got married a month after we met. Oh, Maryann could play emotional games, man. She was able to tap on emotions pretty good." So I look at her. The room around us is still bright with noise and chaos, but I shut it out. How much do I believe? How much of our brand-new friendship is concocted out of thin air and guilt?

27

One afternoon Maryann's best friend – the one named Mariann – dropped by the apartment and went home in tears. It was a defining moment. It was the moment Maryann made a choice. She was forsaking her best friend, someone she'd loved since they were ten years old. She was forsaking this twin because William was drinking beer and saying religion was a crutch and she had to stand by one of them. After he said Mormons were lame and stupid and credulous, that they should learn natural principles, he squashed up his beer can and threw it across the room, which made her mad but what could she do? He said the law of nature was obvious and he was pointing at the plate-glass window as if it framed the universe. "Church people are doing group-think," he told Mariann, and he lay down on the landlady's sofa and covered his face with one bent arm and talked about Ayn Rand and self-interest. It was impressive. He'd read a lot. "You have to create yourself, ladies. But, no, instead you take instruction from the old daddies at church like it was cookies and milk. Which makes you weak. Each and every human on the earthly planet should be acting to self-perfect. Not being an underling or a yes-sayer type."

Mariann knew he was out on parole. But she didn't mention that; she was too polite.

"Just thinking about Jesus about makes me puke," William told her. "You believe he walked out of his grave and flew up to heaven?" He sat up and glared at her as if everything in the world were her fault, as if her stupidity had put him in jail. "I'm not into sacrifice," he told her. He was getting drunk. The can he'd thrown across the room was his sixth or seventh beer in two hours.

Maryann looked at her friend. They both knew that arguing with boys was part of a game. It was a little seductive. They'd both been listening to wild ideas all their lives. It was possible that their parents and teachers and even the elders were wrong. Even the bishop. It was possible that William could answer the secret questioning in her heart. When he said that self-interest is actually a virtue, it made her understand something because she'd watched her mother bend and scrape for everyone else. She'd admired her mother, but William was right when he said if you

take care of your own needs, you do a better job of everything else because she could never be like her mother
anyway and maybe charity is unnatural. Are animals char-
itable? Tigers? Birds? Humans aren't animals, but what
does nature mean to a human being? Her friend was
arguing with William about how God set humans apart,
and when William laughed, Maryann saw her wipe her
face with the heel of her hand and turn away, which made
her feel awful. She noticed when her friend put down her
beer, placing it carefully on a coaster the way she always
did. She heard her say she was going home and she should
have crossed the room then and said something nice but
when her friend left, even then, she didn't run after her or
call the next day because William needed her and a true
friend should know what that means. Need creates duty,
that's what the elders say, but it was the hardest thing in the
world. To choose between them. To watch her best friend
just leave. It was hard, but hard things are strengthening.

The next day she told William that he could try hyp-
notizing her. If it worked, she would expose the truth of
herself. She had nothing to hide. They sat on the floor in
the bedroom and pulled down the shades. When they
were both ready, both sitting face to face, he held his knife
up in front of her and she felt something, a kind of interesting chill. Then William told her to watch the knife,
keep her eyes on it and let herself go. "Like doing it," he

said. "Just relax." He moved the knife back and forth close up to her face while he kept saying Justice was just an instrument, something man-made. He called his knife Justice, like the sword of right, and Maryann went back to the day she had gone out to buy it, how he had sent her off to the store for an eight-inch Buck knife. He sent her to buy it because he was on parole and she went in and purchased the best knife they had in the store and it felt perfect giving him something he wanted when he didn't have anything else. She gave it to him like a present and he asked her to carry it for him because it sealed them. Like in a ceremony. It was strange to name a knife, but William didn't have anything else to name. Not a pet. Not a home or a car or the things that matter to men who are twenty-eight. From now on, she was going to go along with him instead of arguing about every little thing because trust is important. Even if she didn't necessarily believe what he was saying, it helped him to stay calm; it kept his understandable insecurities at bay. Ayn Rand worshipped the great and the exceptional, never the underdog. And look at William. He already had a follow-ing, a network of Randanians. People believed in him and sent him messages and looked after him. He had needed that in jail. And now, with her help, he could go some-place. And as far as the temper went, it was only because he insisted on things. Anyone would do that after jail.

"Did you know why he was in jail?" I asked, breaking in on her story.

"He said it was all a misunderstanding about a gun. Do you want something more to eat?"

For a brief moment, I see Philip's friend Roberto putting his hand into his back pocket. I hear his little gun tap the underside of the table at the dance bar in Guadalajara. Why had he come on my honeymoon? How did he get to be part of my life? It was a big dance bar and I was wearing a black, full-skirted, backless dress with white polka dots. I felt both newly married and sexy, although that feeling did not last through the summer. "Okay, sure." I pick up the plastic bag with the money, my car key, my driver's licence, thinking another coffee would be welcome. I'm really tired. I need a break. It would be comforting to watch the paper cup drop down inside the vending machine and the coffee dribble into the cup. There are moments that bring me close to paralysis, when I start thinking of a particular time that might have gone another way.

"I remember the night the neighbours were burglarized," Maryann says as we cross the floor. She often uses legal-sounding language, as if she reads arrest warrants at night to put herself to sleep. "I came home and there was a police car in the driveway and William was out taking a walk. I found out after we got to Hawaii, the first time he pulled the gun on me, that he was the one that had robbed my neighbour."

But hadn't she said in court that she knew he was travelling with a gun when they left Phoenix? I think about asking, but decide against it. I'm too tired to make sense of anything.

"Anyway," she says, as I'm sliding a dollar into the coffee machine, "the trip was going to be a delayed honeymoon. Bill made it sound romantic."

"Was it?"

"I remember getting off the plane and the air hitting us, all the humidity and the smell of flowers and already, within a few minutes, William started to seem different. I don't know what it was. When we first got there . . . before everything got totally insane, we took the bus out to Hanauma. I remember that. It was spectacular. The clearness of the water. The lushness of the hills. My memories aren't all bad about that place."

I say yes, but I say it in a distracted kind of way because I'm remembering how it felt to have my face in the salty water of that bay. I'm remembering how my brother taught me to use a snorkel, adamant about the pleasure of seeing things from underneath. I'm fourteen years old and I've come out to Hawaii from Kansas, first driving with my parents to California and then getting on a plane for the first time. What I remember about that island is the air:

temperature, moisture, smell. And the nights. They were so intense, I can hardly think of them now.

"We climbed around and explored some of the caves. It was like we were just a normal couple. And we were actually still up there when they cleared the beach that evening. Everyone left and we ended up camping up there. I remember after all the people cleared out, watching a mongoose come out and play on the beach."

"It sounds . . ." I'm thinking, unbelievable, but again the picture, unbidden, forms in my mind. A mongoose, long and thin and sly, peers out from behind a rock, checking for safety, its head moving in suspicious jerks. Maryann is carrying the little Kodak her parents gave her for Christmas. She's watching William watch the animal, putting the camera in front of her face. She's thinking this is what honeymoons are supposed to be. Something to keep in an album, something to remember and look back on in life.

28

That spring, I would visit the prison three times. I was on the right side of the mirror: that's how it felt, surrounded by something familiar, something left over from the phone calls my father used to take while we sat at the dinner table. The phone was so close that we listened, my mother and I, wondering what was being said on the other end of the line. After dinner, my father would take a short nap and then go back to the office. On Saturdays, he was at the office. On Sundays, he was at the office after lunch. And there were those summers when I went to the courthouse with files and ran errands and answered the office phone with a list of the law partners' names.

Around my father, always, there was a sense that, without his immediate attention, matters of importance would fall apart. Wherever he went, my father's briefcase was bulging with work that was overdue. Once, I was taken to the office on a Saturday, when there was no one else around. A couple arrived, not especially young. She was wearing a dark coat and a headscarf tied under her chin. He was carrying his hat, as was proper at the time. My father went out to the hall and came back with a baby, very pink and wrapped up. Young as I was, maybe ten or eleven at that time, I was given the baby to give to the woman in the headscarf. She put out her hands and I handed the baby over. She was wearing red lipstick and she thanked me. As if I'd arranged it. As if I'd given that baby away myself.

So, I went back to the prison, wearing my father's shoes. On my second visit, I was kept waiting outside for several hours, A man who appeared to be ill or exhausted sat outside in the shelter with me. "My sister's in there," he told me, running a hand over his shaved head. "She has six months to live." Across from us was the high double fence with its barbed wire. "We had a lawsuit. Because of the bad medical care." I had to listen hard to catch all the sorrow. The wind was blowing dirt and trash. A woman was sent home to get her baby's birth certificate, which must have a state seal affixed, which cannot be a copy like the one she had brought, although she and the baby come every week. The drive home takes an hour. An hour back.

After an hour of waiting I wandered across the dirt path to the fence. I could see Maryann sitting outside with the Mormon woman who visits her regularly and I shouted to them that I had not been approved yet to come in. Maryann's friend, whose name is Sheron, made a frantic go-away motion with her hands just as a loud speaker blared at me to get back across the road. "She's a good girl," Sheron said, grabbing my arm, when I finally got into the visiting room. "Never gets in trouble and because of you, the guard gives her a warning."

Next came the rush to the vending machines as if they were gods to be pacified. The woman with cancer? "That's Sherrie. Been here since the Eighties. She's had mastectomies, chemotherapy, radiation, but they won't let her out." We were sitting like friends with our soft drinks between us, Sheron having left as I arrived. Now I heard about the wedding and the parents: how Maryann's mother cried on the phone and how both mother and father drove up to Phoenix from Yuma. Father brought a friend. The two older men come into the apartment to talk to William while Maryann goes out with her mother to sit in the car. "Are you getting married because you have to?" I remembered my own mother's words: "And just who is it that you're marrying?" I remembered her reaction. I was running away. Really escaping. I remembered the way she arranged for a cake, flowers, champagne. In spite of everything.

In Phoenix, in the tiny apartment, no one will budge. The men talk for an hour and then exit. But in the morning, Maryann's father calls and says they are still in town. They have not gone home. "I'm going to put Mother on."

"Do you have flowers?" she wants to know. "What do you need?"

Maryann would be married by the bishop in a room off to the side of a church. It would not be the temple wedding of her dreams. She'd wear a wedding dress that William had chosen and after the ceremony he'd call her Mrs. Acker several times to her face.

"That bothered me. I didn't like it."

The good, steady boyfriend off on a business trip.

On her wedding night she is back in her apartment. She sits down by the phone. "I remember that so clearly. We'd been drinking since morning. Bill went to bed. I sat out in the living room by the phone. I had this sudden desire to call Doug. But it was too late. That was the minute I knew I had made a mistake." She looked at me intently. It is a way she has of looking at things. "You know, I was raised that marriage is forever, that you follow your husband. Obedience."

I saw myself crossing the border with Philip, giving my life away. "You ride in the back," my new husband says and I climb in with my girlish white suitcase. His friend Roberto is waiting for us on the other side of the Rio Grande. It's a potent moment, sitting there in the back of a car so dear to me that I used to see it in my dreams. There are Coke bottles and beer bottles and pieces of paper floating around. The smell of old cigarettes. The kittenish sound of the engine as Philip and Roberto chatter away in Spanish and I am swallowed by the dustiest of highways.

Maryann said she was drinking excessively all that day. That's the word she used, *excessively*. "William drove out to a friend's house to borrow a jacket and got lost on the way back. The wedding was at five in the evening. I spent the day running errands and drinking. When I got to the church at 4:30, my parents were already there along with a few guests. Mom was in the church kitchen making a frappé for the reception, saying she only wanted my happiness. She said that if William made me happy, that was enough, but she asked if I wanted to think things through a little longer. Shouldn't I take more time? Then I remember being in the bathroom with my best friend and her asking me if I was sure about getting married to William. I probably said something like once you get to know him and understand him . . . and I remember standing in front of the bishop. I didn't walk down the aisle with Dad. We were all just sitting in the room, then the bishop came in, we stood up and he married us. Then we had the little reception where William would only call me Mrs. Acker."

At the reception people mingled as if the sudden marriage had been a foreseeable event, someone taking pictures, everyone talking. And then it was over, bride and groom taking off to Sizzler's for dinner, the parents driving home to Yuma. Back in the apartment, the groom went to bed and the bride found herself in the dark living room.

I had told her I got married in Arizona. Mentioned the champagne and the cake and the motel with its cactus lit up by the spotlight at the heart of the night. I was still looking for links, but, sitting there with her, I forgot to imagine what it would be like to have no horizon, no sense of context, not to know where the next town is or how big the Alta Dena Dairy is next door, with all those black and white cows living without injury or joy.

29

On the third visit she told me about finding her father. Biological, she called him. A father hears from the child he gave away when she was two months old. She's calling from prison, where she has spent all her adult life. A counsellor had helped her locate him and she had asked another inmate to write to him because, "what if he wanted nothing to do with me? I didn't want to just barge in on his life."

"And your mother, your birth mother?"

"I'm not interested. She's not someone I need to meet."

"Because of being adopted?"

"No, being adopted was fine. I was chosen. I always knew that. It was the best thing to be. It's just that I know what we have in common. She was wild. She was only sixteen when she had me and she already had a three-year-old. Pretty obviously my good side comes from my adopted parents and I know where the other part comes from. I know about nature and nurture. They teach that in here."

"But do you know her name?"

"The thing is, there's so much I have to think about and concentrate on and get done. I have to work on my parole."

I'm looking around at the huge, bleak room we're sitting in. It's enough to drive me crazy, all this grey cement and the row of twinkling vending machines. On one sorry wall, there is a glass case full of baby blankets and small trinkets the prisoners have made. These are for sale, but I have never seen anyone spend so much as a second looking at them. There is, of course, nothing to read. Except the Bible. There is a guard near the door talking on the phone. She is female, but that isn't saying anything. Maryann turns to smile at someone. "Maria. Born in a little village in Mexico and ends up in this place."

I say, "You know while I'm here I thought we could talk about what really happened in Hawaii. We've never talked about that."

She's still looking at Maria. No change in the eyes or face. "You heard my testimony." It isn't a question. "At first I wouldn't even admit things to myself. Not even that

I was present. Not even to my attorney." Then she goes back to Maria, saying she came up with her father when she was sixteen. As if she has answered my question. She says the village where Maria was born had no electricity and no running water, but up here she was more or less abducted by a woman who offered her a job telling her not to tell her family, to keep it for a surprise. Maria was driven straight to an old man's house off in the hills, far from anything she recognized, and the old man told Maria he was a *brujo*. For five long years he raped her and beat her, although Maryann tells this part without emphasis. When somebody killed the old man, Maria was blamed. Maryann opens her hands and looks at her nails while I remember the test we used as girls to see if we were feminine. Open or closed hands. "She gets angry about how naïve she was, but considering the environment in which she was raised, it's understandable, don't you think?"

I say, "And you went off with William for the same reason."

"What do you mean by that?"

"I mean, you were brought up to believe in male authority. Prophets. Doctrines of faith. If Joseph Smith could establish brand-new rules a hundred years ago, why couldn't William Acker do it today?"

Maryann shakes her head. "No. It wasn't that. I truly believed he had a network that would hurt me or my family." She shakes her head again. "I did what he said. It wasn't belief, it was fear. And I was right. When I finally came to my senses and told him to go to hell, that's when he made his first statement about Hawaii in L.A. and started his revenge."

"But, Maryann, in the beginning. That's what I'm talking about."

"I was in love. I was eighteen. I was horny."

"But in Hawaii when he started being different?"

"I still loved him. I was crazy for him. It doesn't make any sense. Even in Phoenix I should have known better. There were signs. One time he saw some man in a car stop and talk to me as I was walking down the street going to the store. Never happened!" She looks down and notices her food, touching it gingerly. "Then in Hawaii . . . one night he went out and I stayed in the apartment and sometime in the middle of the night I felt him grabbing me, yelling about who the man was that just left the apartment." Maryann's face is not easy to read. "He was drunk, but he swore he hadn't been drinking. He swore he saw a man walk out of our apartment and as they passed on the outside stairs, William asked him what he was doing. The man said he'd been in Maryann's apartment. I've heard about people with chemical reactions to alcohol that go way beyond being drunk. Or maybe he was putting on quite the act. Anyway, I had to do some fast thinking and talking to get him to calm down. And the next day when he saw the bruises on my arm and shoulder from where he'd grabbed me, he didn't have a clue where they came from."

"We were going to talk about the crimes," I say, looking over at the clock because I have to leave in an hour. I push my chair back and lean forward to show Maryann that I am here as a friend, that my friendship is serious, but I live in Canada and who knows if I'll ever be back. The metal legs of the chair make a scraping sound on the bare concrete.

"When William turned himself in, you know, he said he was going to cut me loose," she says dreamily. "He said I had nothing to worry about; he wasn't going to let me take the fall. And I was in jail, so instead of co-operating with the detectives, I kept up with the lies he had drilled into my head. To make matters worse, I had a lawyer who had never done defence." She forces a laugh. "He was actually a prosecutor that got assigned to my case."

We aren't talking about the crimes, we're talking about William again. "Before the California trial we were offered a deal by the DA. They would have me plead guilty only to robbery if William would plead guilty to the murder. So, I walked out with William telling me to think about it and when we went into the courtroom a little later, I said, take the deal and he started yelling at me. He called me a bitch and went off in front of the judge, and my attorney requested that our trials be severed. The judge made me waive my rights to a jury trial and about three weeks later I was convicted by that judge under the felony murder rule and within a month William made his first statement about the Hawaii case, blaming me, saying I was the only shooter. I hadn't spoken or written to him since the fight in court, so he cut a deal to testify against me in Hawaii in exchange for immunity. And he ended up pleading no contest to the murder here. I really never dreamed he would go to such extremes. And when he did, I didn't believe anything could possibly come of it; they couldn't use my husband's testimony against me."

"But they changed the law."

"The prosecutor had no case against me without William."

"The DA wanted a conviction. His son was killed the same way." We have been sitting with our food uneaten. We have been talking as if there is no count, no bell that will ring or lights that will flash. Now Maryann looks down at her food again and I wonder if she's waiting for me to eat first, the way people wait for a hostess at a dinner party.

"At times I think he may have set me up," she says quietly, still not moving. "But then, why would he turn himself in? That night when he gave me the car keys and twenty dollars, my only thought was, this is my chance to get away! Then I only got a couple blocks when I got pulled over."

I'm about to bite down on the tortilla and beans, still vaguely warm. No crimes. Only the aftermath. And nothing acknowledged about her childhood. Added to which, the lights are flashing. The count. It takes place in the middle of visiting hours, another humiliation, since the women who have visitors are separated from them and have to line up outside for an hour or more. Visitors stay on the benches close to the vending machines. Talking to each other. Trying to keep children amused. Every inmate in every prison in California is being counted. On my first visit this happened while I was still in the waiting area and it made the waiting that much longer. There is no leaving, either. Once the count starts, doors are on lockdown. On this, my third visit, I have waited an hour and fifteen minutes to see Maryann. Finally I'm inside. We've been talking for less than thirty minutes and now the lights flick off and on.

"I can't stay."

Maryann stands up as if I've pushed her. "Mentally and emotionally I was completely under his influence," she insists, while the narrow bench is between us and people around us are beginning to stir.

"When did you find out about your mother?" I ask.

"Who she really was?" I'm beginning to think that there is nothing to be won. Not any more.

"I was fourteen or so."

"And that was exactly when you started getting wild." We have not even opened our popcorn, but the food will have to be left uneaten. Without a visitor she will have to hurry back to her cell, since she can no longer be in the visiting room.

She smiles. "Linda, I can't say for sure what brought you back into my life at this point, but we have a unique bond, wouldn't you say?" And while the prisoners begin to line up outside, she hugs me. "Linda . . . after so many strange turns, I can't help thinking suspiciously. I instantly began wondering about the woman in the prosecutor's office without even knowing what was said. I think she could have carried your comment about not being sure of my guilt back to the office. Your being a few minutes late could have just been very convenient to their wants. Most people wouldn't think along those lines," Maryann continues, glancing up at the clock, "but there were too many things in Hawaii that just didn't add up until I found out about William's plea bargain. Like, a good lawyer was removed as my counsel and replaced by Hioki." She sighs. "I had him put in a motion to withdraw from my case, but the judge denied it. They were determined to convict me."

We are edging toward the door, stowing our trash. We pass the grandmothers and the mothers being visited. We pass the grandmothers and the mothers visiting. And the children. And the men. I glance at Maria and at the faces of two or three hundred other prisoners. Less than a month before, fourteen dehydrated Mexicans had died near Yuma. Another thirteen barely survived. They'd been wandering for a week in 114-degree heat after being dumped by the "coyotes" who brought them across the Rio Grande. To here.

30

I had no interest in writing to Maryann after that. My interest was all the other way. I wanted the moment of overlap to have meant something to her, but I knew it meant more to me.

I had told her to call. She would have to do that collect.

I transcribed some of the pages of the yellow notebook and sent them to her, even the page where I called her a sullen, brutal bitch. I said maybe together we could try to tell her story. She didn't call. She read the pages and finally wrote back. She said she remembered the man who couldn't be objective because he thought anyone who carried a gun must intend to use it. She said she remembered the blue muumuu, but not the white dress. Then she said that for seven months, in jail in Hawaii, they'd come into her cell every fifteen minutes all night long and shine a light in her eyes. "I learned on the plane going over that William made a bargain with the state, but I wasn't about to kill myself. I'm not the type." She said that her mother wasn't there in the courtroom, that I was right about that.

I went to see my own mother and attended my high-school reunion. Two weeks later, when I was back on the river, I got a message that Maryann had called and would call again. What would we talk about? I thought I could tell her about the reunion. I would turn it into a story, the way I used to turn my life into stories for my mother. It was the way I kept things on track in our house. It was the way I kept my mother happy. I'd tell Maryann I flew down to Topeka and settled in at my mother's right away. I'd tell her that settling in involves taking my bag into the guest room, sniffing and poking at things, then sitting down with her at the dining-room table for a glass of iced tea and some cookies. At this point of the visit we are both shy, I'd say. Only this time my mother had not greeted me at the door. She had not gone into the kitchen for tea while I put my bags down. She was in bed when I arrived and I went to her room and she batted her hand in the dark air around her head. No book in her hand. No television or radio. No interest in me.

The high-school reunion took place at a big new hotel on the fairgrounds. We had a Kansas City band and after two glasses of wine I got into the spirit. The boy I had a crush on all through junior high has a white moustache now. His mother had Alzheimer's and he gave me the name of the place where she lived, but I wasn't paying much attention. Those Topeka boys can dance. I learned with them and we do the same thing on the floor, unlike any other partners I've had. For one of those dancers, I once had a secret name. He married his high-school sweetheart after leaving a first wife, running away to Hawaii, sailing off to the South Pacific. For Maryann, I would make all this appealing.

What do we make of ourselves and how much is circumstance? When I was eighteen I graduated from high school and left home for college. Never wrote to my friends. Burned the first bridge. What a potent year that first one away from home can be; it decides everything. Now I sat at the river's edge, wondering how to tell Maryann the story. I'd tell her that one measures one's changes at such times. "This is what it will be like for you," I'd say. "Every step beyond the prison gate will be a contrast with yourself at eighteen."

But when the call finally came through, she didn't ask about the reunion. She asked about my mother. She sounded worried.

I said I couldn't talk about it. I said something about going home, that it was hard. I had walked two blocks to see my old house, the one where I grew up. Crossed the park and stood there seeing my parents through the windows, young again, my father pounding the table, out of breath. I said, "I used to tell my mother stories. But I think she's maybe past listening." Late night and I am upstairs in my room. My father is back at the office although earlier he and my mother had highballs in the kitchen – he sitting on the yellow stepstool with the evening paper and she dancing between sink and fridge and stove. She had taken her bath, unpinned her hair, put on high heels. He would be home for an hour. For an hour, things would be sexually charged between them. Then it is night and she is downstairs watching television. She is downstairs and I am alone.

"Want to hear the story of my second marriage?"

"Is it good?"

She said she and William were already divorced at the time of the trial in Hawaii, and when she came back to prison in California, Robert was a penpal. First he wrote, then he got approved as a visitor, then he proposed to her. It all happened in six months, but, as Maryann puts it, why would any sane person want to marry someone in prison? She was working as a clerk for her counsellor and asked him about the proposal. Asked her parents too. Maybe her sentence would not go on forever. Maybe she would be out in a few years. Women were actually paroling in those days. Maybe the conviction in Hawaii would not have great consequence. Hioki's appeal was in progress and she was feeling positive. If it now seems unreasonable to imagine sustaining a marriage under such a bizarre circumstance, I have to remember that she longed for a shred of the outside world in an otherwise shattered life, someone to care about her, to visit her, to look after her emotionally. "What do you have to lose?" the counsellor said.

So, a year after the Hawaii case wrapped up, she married Robert in a small room in a corner of the administration building. Her parents were there – a second wedding to be witnessed. Robert's brother and a sister came along and there were five or six inmates who were allowed in as guests.

Afterwards, Robert met Maryann in the visiting room and he stayed for the day. So did her parents. Two weeks later, he arrived for a seventy-two-hour conjugal visit in the Family Living Unit, otherwise known as the FLU. This was the honeymoon. For two years, he came every week and there were conjugal visits every two or three months. But what did she know about him? A bride in prison finds it difficult to ask questions about her new husband's life. He was not like William, this new husband, but he'd done county jail time and he had a brother in prison. He was not unfamiliar with her life.

When his mother died, he came to the prison to tell her. He'd been drinking and doing cocaine. By coming to the prison in that condition, he might have put Maryann under suspicion of bringing drugs inside. So she told him off. "Don't forget, my mama just died!" Robert growled. "And don't forget you're my mama now."

"I told him I was nobody's mama, I was his wife, and if he couldn't get cleaned up, don't bother coming to visit."

So he didn't.

Two years later he sent a money order. No word about where he'd been, or what he'd been doing. Then he arrived. With a question: When could he have a FLU visit? Shortly after that, he vanished along with her legal transcript and a box of her things. Maryann laughed when I said her story wasn't funny. She said, "Next time you do the talking." Her calls are limited to fifteen minutes. They are interrupted by a recorded voice telling us how much time we have left and reminding us that the call is being monitored like every other minute of her life.

I say I will. I promise not to swear. I'll try not to say anything that would reflect badly on her.

TOPEKA

31

That summer, Maryann's parole was denied for the eighth or ninth time. But this time was harder, this time hurt in a different way. Usually the board said she showed no signs of remorse, or she had no insight. They said she still had time to serve on her Hawaii sentence. They said why didn't she just leave William, just walk out the door. But this time she was denied parole when one of the commissioners said he didn't think there was enough time on earth to forgive her. Forgive: to pardon, to overlook, to remit a debt or offence. To be merciful.

She wrote, "So that's it for now. Even though I knew I wouldn't be going anywhere just yet, there was still a small part of me that would have liked to have been found suitable just cuz. Cuz I am; even though no suitability finding means anything right now. And the fact that next year I will have been going to these hearings for 25 years really hit me later that day. Soon I'll be 43. And I wonder when it will end. And what if I don't win this writ in Hawaii . . . Everything just kind of came crashing in on me after the hearing. But I'm working on pulling myself out of it. I have to! I can't let these people get the better of me now!"

I have the transcript from one of her old hearings. It's from July 1992, and the presiding commissioner was Maureen O'Connell, who had presided at William's confessional hearing the year before. Maryann was represented by Deborah Fraser, who had been appointed by the state. Someone from the DA's office was present to represent the State of California, and there were two other commissioners and a correctional officer in the room. The hearing took place at the prison.

O'Connell starts with what she calls Maryann's social history. "You are adopted. Your parents are in Arizona. Your adoptive parents are in Arizona. There's no prior criminal history. You graduated from high school. You got a job in your dad's firm. You met the crime partner, William Acker, got married to him, and then went on a three-week crime spree. There was a string of armed robberies here in California and then the murder. The incident in Hawaii occurred first. You never tried to get away from him?"

MARYANN: Yes, I did try to get away. I left while he was sleeping and I got about two blocks away.

O'CONNELL: So did he beat you after he found you gone?

MARYANN: He just held the gun to me and threatened to kill me if I tried again.

O'CONNELL: Well, you know, I don't hold your ex-husband in much regard because he is one of God's lowliest creatures, but it is unfortunate . . . it's very strange to me. If I was held captive or felt I was a prisoner, I would do anything in my power to get away. You became involved with this guy who was a parolee. You knew that. Two years ago we talked about your parents and why you did all this.

MARYANN: I've thought about it a lot since the last hearing and in the last fourteen years. I've thought about the whole thing a lot and I didn't enjoy being involved in the crimes and I didn't enjoy the intimidation and fear that I felt with him. And I've thought over and over again of trying to figure out maybe there was something different I could have done and I'm still thinking about that and I wish there had been something or I had been thinking more clearly at the time.

O'CONNELL: Well, you know, I'll state it again for the record. I don't think you shot either person. But I think you're still equally as culpable as he is in terms of needing to be punished and taking the lumps for all of the mistakes you made in judgment. My feelings about him are, he snitched everybody off in the State of California and God knows where else, and he left you hanging, holding the bag in Hawaii. But you had an opportunity to fix that and you didn't. And so for the momentary lapse in judgment you are suffering greatly and the ones I feel sorry for are your parents, not your real parents, but your adoptive parents. Those are the ones I feel the most sorry for in this whole mess and of course the victim's family. That's just a total waste, the whole thing. Because clearly you had the correct upbringing, you were taught moral values. You were a churchgoing person. Even if you disagreed with the strictness of the Mormon religion, and your dad and all of that. I heard someone else tell me that not too long ago, and I said you mean to tell me you committed your crime because your father believed in God? Have you told them you're sorry?

MARYANN: Yes, I have. And they have asked me where they went wrong and I have told them over and over they didn't go wrong anywhere. And I am sorry for what I've put them through and I know they've suffered a lot.

O'CONNELL: More than you'll probably ever know.
MARYANN: Probably.

At this point the discussion moves on to Maryann's report card from the prison. She's been discipline-free. She's participated in psychotherapy groups and attended AA and NA groups. She is secretary to the Mexican American Association and has received a two-year college degree.

A second commissioner discusses Maryann's psychiatric report, which states that she has normal posture and gait, normal clothing, personal hygiene, mild to moderate defensiveness, and lack of insight. The second commissioner says, "What do you think Dr. Francis meant by that?"

MARYANN: I'm not sure. I probably do tend to get defensive at times . . .
COMMISSIONER: In terms of your being defensive . . . blaming . . . it appeared to me that your crime partner had a lot to do with the particular crime spree. And you could have left. You could have left in Hawaii and so forth. And you came across kind of like that. But that's my opinion. That's how I saw it. It seemed like it was William Acker's show and you were there for the

ride, but you were kind of scared and so forth. I saw it that way. You don't have to agree with that, but that's how I saw it in terms of how the psychiatrist indicated.

MARYANN: I guess. I'm not saying that I don't accept responsibility. I know I am responsible to a degree for my actions.

COMMISSIONER: You say to a degree. How much to a degree? The conclusion on that report is compulsive personality disorder with passive-aggressiveness and dependent features. It says you appear to be tightly emotionally bound to your parent-child relationship even at the age of thirty-two. It says you are not individuated from your parents. What did Dr. Francis mean by that?

MARYANN: I'm not real sure other than my parents are very important to me.

COMMISSIONER: Maybe you're not an independent thinker. It says here the thrust of psychological development would be to begin addressing your feelings, your self-identity, and your relationship to other people. Dr. Francis says her efforts to get you to go in that direction were analogous to trying to get you to telephone Mars.

The third commissioner discusses various parole plans Maryann has submitted. There is an invitation from her biological father and his wife. There are job offers. The third commissioner says, "Do you know what's happened to your crime partner?"

MARYANN: No I don't. He's in the witness protection program. They're floating him around the United States.

The person from the DA's office makes a statement. She says that all of the crimes appear to have been carried out in a cruel, unfeeling, and calculated manner. She says a perfect example of that was the way the inmate and her crime partner used the last victim's car in the commission of other crimes. She says there was nothing in the file to indicate that Maryann was trying to escape when the police picked her up in Cesario Arauza's car and that, in fact, Maryann appeared to show no remorse at the time of her arrest. "So it is the people's position that she is still a threat to the public safety if she's granted release at this time."

Finally and in conclusion, Maryann's representative, Deborah Fraser, makes a speech. She'd read the article "Where Is William Acker?" in *California Legal Magazine* and told Maryann's family that it might be the means to get her paroled. Now she says, "The district attorney has looked at this case for twenty-four hours. I've been with it for two years since I was first appointed. I've had an opportunity to take a close look at the crime partner, William Acker. I can understand where all of us sort of think that Maryann doesn't articulate real well and it's what to us appears to show a lack of remorse but is actually sort of an aspect of her personality which is not like mine. She is not Italian and she doesn't have that sort of effervescence. But that's Maryann. William Acker is a notorious squeal. He has testified in over thirteen capital cases and he's responsible for sending a man to death row. What's more, during Maryann's trial in California, her attorney was an ex-district attorney and Maryann was his first and last client. At the end of the trial he went back to the DA's office. He didn't even show up for her sentencing. He waived jury in a murder case. That's absurd! And at the time that this trial was going on, the judge was under investigation for making obscene phone calls. . . . This case is real strange. And it's just on and on as weird as it can be. William Acker had told L.A. Detective Ahn about the Hawaii case and said he was doing it so his wife could get psychiatric help. Well, everybody sort of knows when they deal with William Acker that the one person who needs serious psychiatric help is William Acker. He's been in and out of jail since he was six years old. Maryann didn't know that at eighteen. I think we all agree, except perhaps for the district attorney, that Maryann didn't kill anybody. She never murdered a soul and yet she's sitting here for two counts of murder. Now she's got to be responsible for those robberies and at eighteen years old sometimes you don't know your head from a hole in the ground and you don't see a way out. Acker is very good at what he does. I had two cases I dug up where he accused his ex-wife in parcel with another robbery. They dismissed against her. He got a hundred and twenty days. And then six months later he got out, after six months he had another girlfriend try to steal a car in a parking lot in Zody. He tells the cops she did it. She wasn't even near the car. And he ends up doing time and she ends up getting probation. So this guy has got a whole story behind him of accusing other people of doing crimes in which the crime partners have little or nothing to do with it. And this case is no different. What he's done is he's accused his wife of committing two murders and it is on his testimony in Hawaii. How he cut this deal, I don't know. But she ends up going down with a 187 in Hawaii and he walks away with a robbery. He did enough tactical manoeuvres in 1979 at that California trial to avoid ever having to stand trial with Maryann. If he had had to stand trial with her, I don't think she would be here. I think that when the DA talks about no remorse . . . you couldn't describe William Acker better. The man will do anything and sell anybody to save his own soul. In 1991 you were the commissioner on his case when he testified at his own

parole hearing. What's he say? Maryann didn't kill anybody. And he finally . . ."

O'CONNELL: Yes. I asked him the question specifically
and I don't think I was as vehement toward him. I
didn't tell him that he was the scum of the earth at that
time, but he really is.

MS. FRASER: He really is. Is Maryann suitable for
parole? You bet she is. She didn't murder anybody. She's
spent fourteen years in this prison doing time and it
hasn't been wasted. She's raised herself up from being a
stupid kid at eighteen to being at least a decent smart
kid at thirty-two. And I think it's time to let her go. She
should be paroled. And William Acker ought to burn in
hell for putting her here. She does take responsibility
for her crimes, but what does she get? She didn't murder
anybody and that's what she's doing time for. So if you
want to talk about a reasonable risk, if you had to make
a pitch to the governor, this is the one. This is the one.
Maryann Acker is suitable and she should be out.

Soon after the hearing, Deborah Fraser disappeared.
Maryann could not find her. When USC accepted
Maryann's case in 1995, they could not find her. They
needed the files and transcripts from previous hearings.
Where was Deborah Fraser?

Dear Linda,

You want to know something that I am really looking forward to doing when I get out? I want to go grocery shopping. I want to get in a car and go to a store and buy some food and then cook it. And then something else. Going into a bathroom, shutting the door behind me, and taking a shower by myself and barefooted! The shower room, which is at the top of the hall, has three shower stalls and a bathtub. The partitions don't go all the way to the floor, so you get your feet splashed by the water from the other showers. Unless, on a rare occasion there's no one else in there, you can't just get a quiet, peaceful, relaxing shower. And, with 120 people sharing 8 showers (there is a shower room in each hallway), you don't dare go without thongs (shower shoes). And unless you thoroughly scour it before hand, you don't dare take a bath.

I just finished reading The House of Mirth and it struck me how the woman, Lily Bart, made a 'career' out of climbing the social ladder and attempting to find an appropriate husband, all of which led to her demise. Women have come so far in some ways.

Love ya,
Maryann

32

In August 2001, Maryann wrote to tell me that she was making piñatas for the prison's Mexican American Association. The piñatas would be sent to schools and hospitals. There was a banquet planned for September 11. Maryann wrote, "Something fun to look forward to."

Then, when the Trade Center was hit, there was an immediate call. I had thought of her locked away monastically – as separate from news of the outside world as she was from its pleasures. But she listens to the radio at five o'clock every morning and she knew about the attacks before I did. A few minutes after her phone call, the prison yard was closed and the women spent the rest of that day locked down, as if the falling towers had made them suddenly dangerous. While they were on lockdown, more than six thousand dollars was collected among them. "In here it had a unifying effect." Maryann told me, adding that it's their country too. "Our families are out there, remember, and our neighbours, and everything we care about."

It made me want to see my mother.

By late September, airport security had changed – everything had changed – and entering my birth country was a foreign experience. I had become an alien. It takes about seven hours, all told, to get from my front door in Toronto to my mother's Topeka house. I'd fly down, rent a car in Kansas City, and drive for an hour and a half. I'd ring the doorbell. Then, following the greeting, there was supposed to be the sniffing of rooms, the essential iced tea, although all of that had ended a few weeks before when suddenly, like the country around her, my mother had ceased to be recognizable.

At the high-school reunion, I'd learned that several of my old classmates were having similar problems with their parents. I hadn't seen these people for forty years, but they had taken my troubles to heart. I was given business cards, hugs, followup visits in the front yard and the name of that place where the mother with Alzheimer's lived. "It's just what you need," the junior-high crush had assured me. He of the white moustache. I had told him I'd suffered agonies in my great desire for him. We had danced. He was one of the boys with whom I had learned what must have been our unique, local step. He had kindly said, "I wish I'd known."

The other old flame – the one who ran off to the Pacific – offered his legal services. He was the first boy I kissed after my life-changing journey to Hawaii in 1958. I kissed him in the front yard, under the empty flagpole, when I realized that my new attractiveness was flavoured by my desire for escape. Yes, coming back from so far away had given me a little mystery and I clung to it.

The place my reunion dance partner mentioned was nice. I had gone to look at it. There was a second-floor apartment available with balcony doors that looked straight into the branches of an oak, my mother's favourite tree. But how would I ever talk her into it? According to the county social worker, my mother couldn't or didn't feed herself, wash herself, remember dates, or show any interest in life. But she was legally in charge of herself. To go in another direction, to make myself her guardian, would be an indignity I couldn't bear to press on her.

Now, in her dark bedroom, a bundle of blankets was unresponsive. "Linda's here," said Sandee, who was employed by the county to be there every afternoon. The smell of uneaten chicken soup filtered in from the kitchen.

Mother rolled over and smiled, then rolled into her fetal position again.

"We're going to the hospital," I said nervously.

Mother said, "Not today. I don't feel well enough."

I cursed my brother for his plane crash. I wrung my hands and bit my lips and went in the living room and paced. Then I told Mother to get in my rented car or I would call an ambulance.

She locked herself in the bathroom, but came out twenty minutes later lipsticked and powdered and rouged. "My clothes . . ."

"You'll go in your robe." Sandee and I led Mother outside, all the way to the curb where I had parked my car. She seemed to be treading very carefully, as if there were hundreds of eggs on the grass. Or land mines. From the height of the curb the passenger seat seemed to be miles away. We lowered her into it.

I didn't think that she was never coming back. I didn't think that she would be assigned to the locked mental ward of the hospital. I thought I was doing my best and maybe I was. In her room in the mental ward there was a mirror, a dressing table, a closet, a private toilet and wash-basin. I kept thinking of prison, but Mother thought she was in a hotel.

Maryann called but what news could she have that was equal to this? "If it would help at all to talk," she said. She said how much she regretted not being there with her parents when they were sick, when they needed her.

"I'm trying," I said. "But I live in another country." I was thinking of the months Mother had spent with me in Hawaii – a middle-aged widow and a young divorcee trying to be a family for two little girls. I wanted to tell Maryann how much I was missing my mother, but how could I explain the force she had been in my life?

"I wish you would describe her," Maryann said.

"Her pride and joy is her cat, Miss Pym," I said, "but when I'm at the hospital, she never mentions her."

So Maryann told me about Nermal. She had been working for Inmate Day Labor, the prison construction crew where she was a clerk, keeping records of materials and orders for her boss, while the other women prisoners did electrical or plumbing or building work. This has been her favourite job, but it's not dependable because state projects often run out of money. The central unit needs a new roof, but that will have to wait. A housing unit needs to be rewired, but there is nothing in the budget for it. Still, prisoners have to work. They need money for tampons and shampoo and soap. They need money for food from the canteen and for pyjamas and underwear. Stamps. Stationery. Besides, it's the law. Each of them has a five-day workweek, with the average pay being thirty-five cents an hour, although they never see any money; they have accounts that they draw against, the way coal miners used to draw against supplies at the company store.

It was while working for Inmate Day Labor that Maryann met the little cat named Nermal – "because he's not quite normal" – one of the many feral cats who lived on the prison grounds. Nermal had started watching Maryann during work hours, when the rest of the crew was outside. "I'd feed her lunch meat out of my box lunch because generally I won't touch the stuff anyway." Naturally the little cat followed Maryann to the next job site. Every morning she'd wait for her generous human friend at the gate they had to go through to get to work. When IDL completed the project and relocated, someone told Maryann that the cat was still waiting at the gate.

One day Maryann was sent back to that site to pick up some tools. She called and the little cat came running. Maryann took her to the new site, and she and Valere started showing her the way to their housing unit until Nermal took up residence on the meagre windowsill of their cell. She said, "Now, about Miss Pym," and I tried to imagine her face, although I had no idea where she was sitting or standing. I couldn't imagine what it looked like where she lived. "Once I dreamed that I was getting ready to parole," she said. "I was trying to put Nermal into a box to take him with me, but before I could get the lid on

the box, he jumped out and wouldn't come back. Linda,
I was devastated."

I was following the story. It was a little diversion,
nothing more, and our minutes were ticking away. Then
she said that when the prison decided to cull the cats, she
got frightened. There had always been rules. No pets for
prisoners. No taming. No feeding. But now the ones they
could find were going to be killed and for the first time
in days, I focused on something besides my mother or
myself. When she said she had wangled permission to get
Nermal out, I listened. She had arranged for permission to
give her cat to Sheron, the faithful visitor. It was a sacrifice. To guarantee his safety. She took a long breath.

33

At the hospital, a woman named Velma invited me to sit down at the bingo table where she and my mother were sitting. My mother, never a player of games, sat there listlessly while Velma was bouncy, imparting real urgency to the game. She took an interest in Mother, tracing her background and mentioning a friend they had in common. "Why Jill Seegram! She's from my town."

At the mention of Jill Seegram, Mother's face brightened a shade.

"Why I remember their place," Velma insisted. "That apartment over the store. They had some real good antiques."

"Jill always looked so refined," I added next. "With that ash-blond chignon. And her tweeds." There had been rumours about Jill and my father.

"Exactly!" Velma exclaimed. "But she's dead now," she added respectfully, gazing at Mother. "You sure couldn't be her age."

Both of these assertions threw Mother back into confusion. These days she is frank about her age, although it took ninety years to make her so. Finally, she realized she could use it as an excuse. "I'm an old lady, for heaven's sake. It's fine if I want to stay in bed." When Mother told Velma her age, Velma said, "I don't believe it! Isn't she something?"

I remembered being driven down to the Seegrams' apartment on a Sunday afternoon, since that was the only day of the week my father spent any time with us. The apartment was huge, full of furniture that looked impressive in the dusty light. But something was wrong in that place. An old man and a beautiful wife. "You went to England with Jill after Dad died," I reminded my mother.

Now she looked at me. Really looked. "Yes, I did," she agreed. "She smoked all the time. Yes, that's right."

There were only certain hours I was allowed to visit my mother, so I spent the rest of my time going through her house, as if my attention to her basement, her desk, her closets would bring her back to herself. I made piles. To throw away, to give away, to clean. Big bigger biggest. The closets were a heap of various vintages, thousands of shoes, mouse droppings, dead mice. At 2:20 I'd dash to the car and drive to the hospital, where I'd find Mother with Velma, although Velma's husband was often sitting nearby. All the ladies in the mental ward eyed him hungrily. "I'd like one of those," my mother whispered to me. Later it was simply, "I want him."

I told Mother that Miss Pym had been hiding in the closet and she looked at me blankly. "I don't know what kind of hotel this is," she whispered. "Last night a big black girl just came right into my room." This with a snort of disbelief.

"It's a hospital," I would say, during conversations like this.

"Why would I be in a hospital? There's nothing wrong with me."

"Remember how tired you've been? You've been flat in bed for six weeks."

"That's a lie."

In our family there was a current of popular language that never saw the light of day. Mother would say, "Linda Jane, don't fib." Her strongest word of censure was "That's vulgar," the lowest jibe. So this was a new departure, a new uncensored mother. "Anyway, I'm going home tomorrow. They're not doing anything for me here."

"But I saw your schedule on the board. You had Exercise this morning and a group meeting. You worked with leather."

"I hated that. Imagine, with all the things I've done in my life, and I couldn't lace that silly shoe."

Velma had been standing in the doorway. Now she entered the room and patted Mother's knee. "Leather's hard," she acknowledged. "It's a whole different skill from other things."

Mother was right about the things she'd done in her life. In the closet, I found Miller shoes, delicious fruited hats, and beautiful sweaters, many of them knit, purled, lined, and decorated by my mother. I could remember occasions for each of her outfits – skirt, blouse, jumper, coat – all made by a dressmaker to be arranged and rearranged. As a girl, evaluating the many possibilities as with paper dolls, I was entranced. No store-bought clothes came near the imaginative variations or style of my mother's wardrobe. A pair of alligator pumps on platform soles. A matching purse. These were treasures that could not be traded, sold, given, or trashed. But I went on filling clear plastic bags because over the past several years, whether because of failing eyesight, failing nerves, or despair, Mother's excellent housekeeping skills had disappeared. The evidence of neglect was there in the closet, where several small creatures had died, no doubt miserably, and where I found small bones and cobwebs and unsorted papers and every cancelled cheque ever signed by my father going back to the 1930s. Once I had filled the plastic bags, I washed the shelves and began to reconstruct the closet as it might have been. My favourite dresses were rehung. Several pairs of shoes in their original boxes were put back on the upper shelf. Bags were arranged, even ornaments. It was a memorial to my mother made of her own artifacts.

She kept an old footstool in that closet – a wooden box with an upholstered lid and a slipcover. Over the years she had used it to hide her silverware and her jewellery. "Who would bother to look in it?" she'd always say, and now opening it felt like a case of bad manners – as if she might suddenly jump in her Oldsmobile and drive home, sweep through the door carrying groceries, the dry cleaning, the mail, and find me *en flagrante.*

"Oh my God! Sandee! Come in here!"

Sandee was cleaning the kitchen shelves. She waded through the dining room, into the bedroom, past the bureau, and over to me. "A .357 Magnum," she intoned, with a big intake of breath. "Beautiful!"

The last of my father's guns.

"You could take it to the cops."

"No way."

Dying with his boots on, collapsing of a heart attack during a courtroom argument (defending a client he distrusted and disliked), my father had left a legacy of thirteen loaded guns. *Spell spaghetti. Seventeen times thirty-eight.* Holding his gun put my father's voice into my head and my hand began to shake. "I'm sure it's not registered. Anyway, they'd sell it." Raised to be more suspicious of cops than of robbers, I tucked the gun back into its sheepskin holster and told Sandee about the day my brother had taken us – what was left of the family – out to Mission Creek, which ran through a piece of land my father bought when he was already out of money or time to build on it. My father had planned to erect an adobe house there, brick by handmade brick. Skip told Mother to choose one of the thirteen guns and, while children and grandchildren watched, she chose her weapon, loaded it, and took aim at a log that was bobbing along in the muddy water of Mission Creek. I have a photograph of this moment – Esta's wide eyes and my brother with his shirt off, looking straight ahead as if we were proving ourselves against a common enemy, although the only one we shared was Death.

"You never tell me anything," I'd heard Velma say to Mother. And I might have said the same. The rumours about Jill Seegram and all the others, even the mother of that boy in my class. My father's ward. I used to imagine that he was a brother and maybe he was. Maybe he was a secret my father and I kept, like the clients he visited when I was in the car with him, broken women, chain-smoking. "Your father was crazy about you," is what Mother used to tell me, as if any failure of affection between us was mine. She never complained about his temper and seemed not to notice that he terrified and humiliated me, that I was expected, at all hours, to be without blemish, to perform on demand. *Spell pragmatic. Now! Sound it out.* In his presence, I'd make myself small, being careful not to give him reason to notice me. *Do you want to come inside for your spanking or take it out here in front of your friends?* Hearing his car in the driveway, I'd go to my bathroom and lock the door. Sometimes I'd be sick. "I have nothing to tell," is what Mother would say to Velma. "I'm a happy person except for being here." But while she was there, propped up in her hospital bed, I suddenly wanted to shout at her. Lies! Lies lies lies!

What had come over me? I wanted to shake this mother who had kept herself blind and silent. I wanted to expose an old woman who was too far gone to defend herself. All my life I had wanted only to make her happy, but her happiness depended on something entirely false. I remembered, while she was in that bed that was wound up like a beach chair, that she had made me promise to stop seeing my college friends. A particular boy. I was hurting her reputation. "What you do in Boulder gets back to Topeka, don't forget," she'd told me. She and my father had driven across the whole state of Kansas and into the mountains to deliver this message. It was then that I made my call to Mexico. It was after that afternoon that I ran away with Philip. I could never go home again, not to a mother who would demand such a sacrifice.

"We have your mother on a new medication," one of the nurses announced later that day. "These things work their wonders fast in the elderly."

The next day, I rented the apartment that looked right into the branches of the tall oak tree. The wonder of people, like stories, is that they are mutable, or so I like to think. When ten days had passed and I walked Mother out of the locked ward and into the elevator, she had gone down the darkest hole of her life and come out the other side. She said she was ready to go home, and I said, "We're going to your new apartment. With a nice tree and birds."

"I need to go home first and get my clothes. And what about Miss Pym?"

I told her the cat, all her clothes, her books, her furniture were waiting at the new address and we drove there without incident, without passing Go or collecting two hundred dollars or bursting into tears. Mother looked out the passenger side of the car at the town she had adopted seventy years before. She watched it go by. And at her new door, one she had never entered before, she invited me in for iced tea.

34

That gun of my father's was a beautiful object perhaps, but it was something I wanted not to exist, as I want all guns not to exist. Anyway, I would never be able to bring it back to Canada, where handguns are prohibited, just as they should be.

As if my father's spirit were embedded in the gun, I could feel its weight all that week, while Mother was settling into the apartment and I slept in her more or less empty house. Knowing the gun was there, in the closet, full of my father, I did not feel safe. Knowing the decision of what to do with it was mine to make, and that my father was somehow involved, I actually could not sleep. There must be a right answer. Where my father was concerned, there was always a right answer. And my problem, eternal, was to find it.

Word problems, tests. I began to wonder what had happened to the other guns – twelve – that he had left in various places when he died. Under the front seat of his Lincoln, in the basement, in the linen cupboard . . . and where else? I wondered why he had wanted so many guns – a man who believed they were useful for one purpose only. "Never pick up a gun unless you intend to use it. Never shoot unless you intend to kill."

Like that man on the jury, Mr. Sugai.

My father kept a gun in his handkerchief drawer.

"Is it loaded, Daddy?"

"Of course it is."

I used to put his handkerchiefs away after they were ironed. I used to touch the strange skin of this gun. I used to watch my father get dressed in the morning, putting on his undershirt first and then his socks. Boxers, starched shirt, suit pants, tie. Always the same. Order. Finally the jacket. And nakedness always part of our family life. I watched him open and shut the drawer. Unfold a handkerchief. Tuck it and his wallet into the right back pocket.

It didn't occur to me until years later that only when one of us was naked did I feel safe. At those moments, we were like dogs with our bellies exposed. Paws up. You don't ask a naked girl to do arithmetic. Peeling the vegetables, cleaning the sink, sweeping, or vacuuming, I was bound to irritate. It was while vacuuming that I finally rebelled. There had been a dinner party the night before and I was put to cleaning the Oriental rug before we went out someplace. A long drive, I think it was going to be.

The table had been shoved off the rug. It sat, large and polished in an unusual situation, relegated to the margins of the room. I had followed orders. Had pulled the vacuum quietly in from the broom cupboard near the back door. I was wearing a full skirt, already dressed for our departure. Dressed up, because that was the way things were in those days. One of my duties was to be pretty. Smile. Stand up straight. Walk with my shoulders back, toes forward. Once, I had mentioned to my father that ballerinas walk with toes angled out, but my father said, "Nonsense," and kept his eyes on my feet.

I was prepared for constant scrutiny; it was a fact of life. Maybe, on some level, I was even prepared for the rage that boiled up in my father when he saw me plug the old Hoover in and start across the rug with it. Anyway, I should have known it was coming. I was doing something he had told me to do, but I was doing it wrong, as always and usual. Still, I pushed the vacuum. Back and forth, back and forth. I pushed and pulled until my father grabbed the handle and yanked it away. *This instant. Right this minute! Do it correctly!* Beside himself, if that phrase means what I think it means. But when I tried again, pushing and pulling, every swipe was worse, more terrible, more a blow to what he knew vacuuming ought to be. He stood there shouting and grabbing, but I could not get it right. I was too fast. Too slow. I was pushing randomly. I wasn't pulling back all the way. My crying always made things worse, so I tried to control my breath, but the tears were starting. No show of emotion! He wouldn't stand for it. "I'll give you something to cry about." He grabbed and shouted and squeezed until I sank to my knees, skirt billowing out, face on the rug – colours I knew from rolling around down there with our dog.

It was the only protest I had ever made, but it ended something.

I refused to get up.

My mother fled upstairs and sat in a chair in the guest room, where she never sat. She was crying. "I don't like you. Either of you."

Now, as I tried to sleep alone in my mother's house with my father's gun, so many images came back from the past that I'd get up and drink a glass of milk and begin to attack her library. Because, if my father had guns, my mother had books. There were mysteries, art books, cookbooks, novels, and histories. The political lives of FDR, Truman, and Adlai Stevenson, her heroes. Anthropology, Biblical scholarship, decorative design and ballet. I tried to sort

them and then gave up. I told people to drop by and take
some home. I called the library.

I solved the gun problem privately. All by myself, I took
an evening drive. It felt appropriate, once I had thought of
it, because my father had a sailboat that was the love of his
life. The truth is that most of the time, year after year, it
was in dry dock in our garage. My boyfriend helped sand
it. My brother helped sand it. My father worked on it at
odd hours of the night to ease the pain in his back from a
war injury. The boat was wood, a Thistle, designed in
Scotland. And it was decidedly the fastest, definitely the
loveliest boat on Lake Shawnee. But when my father got
elected to the schoolboard, there was no time for sanding
and the boat developed a serious case of dry rot, which
meant it was never where it was designed to be. For years
we stored yard equipment and grass seed in its shapely hull
and it became a not very funny family joke. But I remember a few hours of early childhood when riding the surface
of the lake brought me close to bliss. My father had made
me a seat up in the bow and we often sailed at night, when
I could feel the swell of wind from the billowing jib sail
and count the comforting rhythm of the flashing red and
green warning light. Up there, riding the dark surface of

the lake, I was under his protection but happily out of reach. My father directed his temper at the sails and lines.

It was therefore a sort of tribute, a kind of memorial to my father, when I heaved the last of his guns – the beautiful .357 Magnum – into the water near a place where the boat had been moored in the years before I started fourth grade. I watched it sink. I could not throw the gun very far and the water was not very deep. Wondering whether some bad person might see it or find it or fish it up and put it to evil use, I hovered at the shoreline. I felt slightly silly. I felt apologetic. It seemed to me that I should apologize to my father. It seemed to me that I should indulge in an appropriate rite. Eventually, though, I turned on my heels and went back to my rented car. There is very little to be said about such events. As I drove away, travelling the bumpy road we had driven so many times, so many years ago, I had to admit to myself that throwing the gun in the lake was not a tribute to my father, but exactly the opposite. I had buried his gun in the waters of Lake Shawnee out of spite.

35

Maryann's father was born a Baptist, like mine, but when Maryann talked about him, I felt jealous. He came into his manhood during the Depression, like my father did, and while my father was selling silk stockings door to door, Bert was selling tires in east Texas. He was also paid to collect on bills when drought, dust storms, and wind took out three wheat crops in a row. He'd hoped to be a pharmacist, but when he was still a boy his father died and he went to work for the family. That was his character. And near the end of his life, he typed out a letter on fifteen single-spaced pages for his surviving children and for his three grandchildren, for whom he must still have felt some shred of hope. Penne found the letter after he died and sent a copy to Maryann. The sentences run off the paper at the bottom, but Maryann says that is just like her father, who refused to waste anything, even space.

"Sometimes I would encounter a distraught and angry farmer," he wrote about the years he spent collecting on bills. "I have been run off with a shotgun, hay hook, and fence post. I would drive my truck into his yard, turn it around leave the engine running, both doors open and by this strategy could get away with a whole skin."

When things dried up completely, Bert decided to join the great exodus to California, but he stopped in Phoenix on the way. It was 1939, and he looked around at the town. It was a whole lot better than east Texas and he found a job there pretty easily, riding the bus from Mesa into Phoenix every morning, taking the route that Doug must have taken to visit Maryann's apartment in 1978. "There was a real cute girl who rode the bus from Mesa. I wanted to get acquainted with her but had a problem as she always sat with her girl friend and I had difficulty talking to her. I finally got a break. Her friend was ill one day and she saved me a seat by her. She denies she saved me the seat but I don't believe her."

When Gladys moved to Phoenix, she was "much more available for serious romance and I tried to sweep her off her feet. Didn't work out that way she was a serious conservative lovely Mormon girl and made me use all my skill to convince her I was her knight in shining armor."

They went to movies. They went to dances. At the end of an evening out, they would pass her house and keep walking two more blocks to a coffee shop where they could talk the rest of the night. "I decided if I was ever to get enough sleep to stay alive I had to change my tactics and see if the woman would marry me."

On December 7, 1940, they began married life in a small apartment. A baby boy was born a month before Pearl Harbor and they named him Butch. He was to provide them with a bonding tragedy. As I read the letter written so many years later, I am alert to Bert's casual dismissal of disaster and his joking references. Although the baby's death, which was caused by a paper clip that pierced his throat, must have caused unfathomable heartbreak, Maryann's father does not betray his feelings. There was an infection. The child was six months old. Then there is this: "Gladys was and is a life long member of the Church of Jesus Christ of Latter Day Saints and believing that Butch would be returned to her to raise in the millennium helped her to overcome the terrible loss and face the future with hope. She convinced me this was true and it helped me too. We took up our lives and walked straight into WW2."

Bert and my father were both in the navy, stationed in the Philippines. It seems possible that they knew each other there. It's a coincidence that I cannot help imagining. I have a folded piece of paper on my desk – a memento of that time. It's the menu for Christmas dinner, 1944 – a drawing of candles lighting up the word *Liberation*. *After Three Years* is written underneath the candles. And *In the Philippines*. The dinner began with an orange basket and chilled tomato juice. There were olives, sweet mixed-pickle relish, pineapple and cheese salad, turkey supreme soup, and roasted tom turkey with sage dressing and giblet gravy. There were snowflake potatoes, cranberry sauce, buttered carrots, and peas. There were roasted sweet potatoes, whole kernel corn, and Parker House rolls. Chocolate milk, demitasse, hard candy, and "home baked" pumpkin pie. To the left of the menu, my father collected a group of signatures. A few are indecipherable, but right in the middle is the signature of Douglas MacArthur, who has written underneath, *May God preserve and protect you all – is my Christmas prayer*. I've searched among the names for Bert Bray's and while I can't see it, I like to imagine him there.

At that time, I was barely alive and Maryann was a long way from being born. Gladys had given birth to a second son a few months after Bert shipped out. When he left Australia for New Guinea, he was located in a place where the Japanese had been entrenched. "I still remember their privy," he writes. "It was built of split bamboo with a floor of bamboo over the holes in the ground. The holes in the floor were cut square and the edges were neatly laced with bamboo and covered with bamboo mats. Between each hole, a two-foot-high curtain of woven grass was hung. I thought that was pretty neat compared to a slit trench the GIs sometimes used."

I have a tiny photograph of a man from New Guinea left among my father's papers. The man is bare-chested, with wild, starchy hair. There is a note on the back: *man of the admiralties*. Maybe our fathers met out there in the aboriginal Pacific. And then, back in Manila in June 1945, they might have met all over again as they were being shipped out. In September, Bert's outfit was decommissioned and he went home through Hawaii, just as my father did. It was in Hawaii, jumping to the ground from his plane and then catching his heavy pack, that my father sustained his only apparent war injury. Two weeks in Pearl Harbor and Maryann still so far in the future that a small stitch in time might have changed everything. If she'd been born an hour later, a day later . . . if she'd been given to another family . . . if Gladys and Bert had divorced . . . if Bert had been killed . . . if the second son had not died . . . Larry Hasker would still be alive. And Cesario Arauza, as well. But Gladys met Bert in L.A., where they had a brief second honeymoon. They danced at the Paladium Ball Room, visited the beach, and wandered around hand in hand. It was exactly the kind of honeymoon Maryann would try to replay with William.

I wonder if Bert's new son met his father the way I met mine, by locking myself in the upstairs bathroom the day he came home from the war. "I found a strange thing had happened to me," Bert writes. "I couldn't make a decision. Having all my thinking done for me by the navy for three years had impeded the process of thinking things through and reaching a decision," Bert went back to work as a salesman for McKesson, working the streets of Phoenix. In his letter, he calls himself an honest con man. "I have tried many times to explain my fascination with selling and the only explanation I could verbalize is it is great sport to get an intelligent man to spend his money for my products. It is a one on one contest usually played on his turf." Gladys was working three days a week and they managed to pay off the bills that had resulted from Butch's accident and death.

Penne was born in 1950, the same year William Acker was born in Illinois. Brother Mike, the second son, had developed asthma when he was two or three years old, but by the time he was twelve, he was playing shortstop on a baseball team while Bert coached. Consummate father, he had been active in the Mormon Church since his marriage to Gladys, but it was Mike's death, at the age of fourteen, that made him decide to be baptized.

The daughters Bert writes his letter to actually number three. He says: "I need to include a paragraph about two other members of our family I have not touched on. About two or three months after Mikes passing Gladys came home with a two month baby girl. This came about through a friend Mary Sorsenson. She was a court clerk and heard of this baby girl being put up for adoption and decided we needed a baby to replace our sons. She sure put our minds to thinking in a different direction and helped us over the hard spots. Penne was missing Mike a lot and found some solace in coping with a new baby sister. She like Mike before her thought we were replacing her in our affections with the baby. She came to know better and helped Gladys cope with the new child in our lives. The other member I mentioned was Polly, a Navajo girl we received in our home on the Indian placement program of the Church. We had her three years and learned to love her a great deal. We still hear from her once in a while. I want my daughters to know I am proud to be known as their father and I love them very much. I admire their spirit and the way they strive to cope with life and its blessings and problems. I am going to leave the telling of their life story to them and explain I realize I have wrote more about the boys than the girls not because I found their lives less interesting or compelling but they are still here to write of their own. I encourage them to keep a journal which will make writing their history much easier and more complete. I would doubly encourage my Grand Children start now and keep a journal all their lives. I want Brandy, Jess, and Shannon to know I love them and am proud of them. I would ask them always to remember they are Heavenly Fathers children and He wants them to develop the talents he has given them and live clean lives that they may return to his kingdom and dwell there with Him and their Grandparents and parents forever."

At the time of Bert's letter, Maryann had been in prison for twenty years.

36

Yuma was a town of 25,000 souls in the southwest corner of Arizona when Maryann was living there. The Mormon Church had divided it into stakes, as it divides every town and city into stakes. It had divided the stakes into wards, as it always does. Yuma, on the east bank of the Colorado River near the confluence of the Gila, was deep in Mormon country, Mormon mentality. Regulation, regulation, discipline. Prayers and authority and long, weird underwear. Growing up in a family in which the notion of Mormons as the chosen people permeated every minute of life. Maryann's hold on identity must have been tenuous. Maybe biology is destiny, she must have thought. Her mother had abandoned her. Her father had given her away. Maybe all her attempts to be worthy were fraudulent. But her new parents kept insisting that she had been sent to earth to choose between right and wrong, that she had the earthly treasure of free will. If she could manage to live according to God's law, all of them, including the two dead brothers she had never met, would be together in the Millennium. It was up to her.

Of course she wanted to help her family live together eternally.

If she could only hold things together.

"I felt huge pressure," she says now. "I had to make up for everything – my brothers' dying and my sister ruining everything for our family." In Yuma, there was something – a meeting of the youth group, a stake dance or a ward dance or a society meeting – every night of the week. But in Yuma, there were also kids who hung out at the river. "I started ditching school quite a bit. My parents tried to set limits for me, but I ignored them and did what I wanted and when Mother gave me her Volkswagen, it got worse. Once, I was driving away from school on my way to the river and I passed my dad. I had to make up a story, but I was getting good at that."

Living in preparation for the second coming of Christ, one doesn't question the bishop, or the elders in the church, but Maryann began to question those closer to hand. Why did she have to believe everything she was told? Why not ask a few questions? Such as who was Joseph Smith? What made him so special? Why shouldn't he be considered a lunatic? Are we born the way we are or is there a chance to change?

Bert and Gladys prayed for their child. They argued with her, but there was a side to her they couldn't reach. Why tell her about the wild mother who gave her away, if not as a warning? And how to discipline her? "I was spoiled," Maryann admits.

She got her first job as a cashier, then a second job as a salesperson at the new JCPenney. When she got laid off there, she went to work at Kmart and one night, when she was coming home from work, she got rear-ended at a stoplight. Because of a whiplash injury, her parents' insurance agent wrote her a cheque and she decided to take a vacation and visit an aunt and uncle in San Jose. "I actually contemplated moving up there. Probably should have. Instead, I went back."

I tell Maryann there are a hundred things I would rewrite in my life, almost from the beginning. And there are things I would give myself, including an ounce of her confidence in fate. "My first job was at JCPenney too," I announced one night when she called. "Isn't that strange? There are so many similar things in our lives."

"Did you get laid off?"

"I did. I only lasted a week. And I never shopped there after that. I went to work in my father's office from then on, every vacation. He said we might as well keep the money in the family, even though I never understood what he meant exactly. Unless it meant I couldn't contribute from the outside."

"Did you want to be a lawyer?"

"I wanted to be an architect, like my brother. But I was a girl. My parents thought I should learn stenography, in case I didn't get married or my husband died in some tragedy. You know, psychologists say kids who feel abandoned are excessively dependent. On boyfriends. Husbands. Did you know that?" Sometimes I spent entire phone conversations doing this, looking for things that made sense of her life or offered some sense of connection between us. JCPenney. Fathers. Yuma. "My great-grandfather went out there and tried to settle a land claim." With each discovery it was as if I had come upon some proof. We have a unique bond, Maryann had said, that last afternoon in the prison visiting room, but I could tell that she was not really interested in the little links I forged. Again and again, I asked Maryann to tell me about the house where she lived in Phoenix, "growing up, when you were still happy. I know you don't want to go back, but I think something must have happened there that made William the next part of your life." I didn't say that the freedom of a girl who leaves home at seventeen is not really freedom, not for a while, not while she is running away. A woman who is desired feels powerful, but a girl who leaves home at seventeen is bound to carry everything she's fled: authority, control.

The weight of it.

In that girlish white suitcase!

And what she finds is not independence but another authority. What she finds will challenge everything she was taught to believe.

I was a nice woman in a foreign country who was taking an interest in her. It seemed to suffice, but then sufficiency is relative and Maryann had her own secrets.

It was at Kmart, in her senior year of high school, that Maryann met the man she abandoned for William. "Six foot two, with sandy brown hair. But what attracted me was how gentle he was, taking pictures of kids." Doug went from store to store, town to town. He worked in Kmart and other places. He lived in a suburb of Phoenix and that settled it. Maryann told her parents she would not be going to Arizona Western, the junior college in Yuma, although they had offered to pay her tuition there. Instead, at the age of seventeen, she drove off in a car that had been her mother's. "I was hell-bent on getting back to Phoenix."

Which was easy for me to understand. I remember kissing my high-school boyfriend goodbye when I left for college. We promised each other all kinds of things but I was hell-bent too. Away from Home. That's where I wanted to be. I went away to school and fell in with a group of strangers. I was free of my mother. I was free of my father. I didn't know I would never go back.

And there she is out in her driveway on an evening when she is still seventeen. There is a warm breeze. She's sitting in the little Volkswagen. There is a six-pack in the trunk and a pack of cigarettes in her purse and the breeze is a song coming through the trees. She's turning on the radio, waving to her mother, who stands at the window. Goodbye! Her mother partly hidden by the fluffy curtain. She's looking furtive.

Maryann was president of the Young Adult Group at church, where she took Doug to dances. "Were you in love?"

"Not enough."

"But you thought you were."

"Not enough. Not enough."

"But . . ."

"I thought we'd get married eventually."

Doug had spent two years in South America on his mission, but he was living with his parents again. When Maryann moved to Phoenix, they saw each other whenever he was in town. He was twenty-five. A nice man. Good to her. When he was gone, she went out with other men. She also went out with Mariann and Lisa and someone named Lori. She had an apartment, a job. Father, mother. Church. Support from all sides.

37

I spent the summer of 2002 sitting at the table where I'd first written to Maryann two years before, watching three new robin hatchlings squeeze each other against the edges of their nest. I had just come back from another visit to New York, where it had seemed important to stand at the brink of Ground Zero and stare into the massive hole where the Twin Towers had once stood. I wanted to grapple with it for myself and for Maryann, who could not visit the pit with its trucks and cranes. It was an ugly pit except for the sheets of weathered paper covered in plastic and hung on a surrounding chain-link fence. Remember Me . . . name, age, photograph. The flowers and mementoes were pretty well abused by a long winter and a great many tears. And there was no particular order to anything. A man in a hard hat spoke Polish to a group of listeners. A man sweeping a marble stairway told me that yes, I was in part of the original building . . . where there were still signs pointing to elevators and restaurants that no longer exist.

While I was away Maryann had been trying to call. There were messages left in both English and Spanish. *You have a call from an inmate in a California State Prison . . . quien es un preso de una facilidad . . . If you do not want to receive this call, press 7 . . . If you never want to receive a call from this institution again, press 6 . . . If you accept the charges for this call, press 5 . . .* What she wanted was to tell me about seeing an old video of her parents.

The video had been made the year after Maryann's Hawaii trial. She was told about it by another prisoner who worked for In Service Training, where they had been going through the old video files. This one had been made by a television station for a program about California prisons. Maryann and her parents were in a segment on the Family Visiting Program. "I had never seen it," she told me when we finally connected. "And I didn't see the whole thing, but of the people I saw in the video, there are only three of us still in this facility. There was one gal named Goldie, who had probably been here for a couple of years when this was done. They asked her how long she would be here and she said 1985, which is exactly what I thought too, because at that time, we still believed we'd get out at our minimum eligible parole date." Maryann's voice sounded dry. No wonder. In 1983 she was sure she had only another two years in prison. "She's still here for killing a man who was molesting her infant daughter," Maryann whispered. "We're both still here."

The video was hard to watch. "I don't even know that I can put into words how it affected me. The first flash of Mom actually took me by surprise. I almost didn't recognize her. Her voice, when she began to speak, sounded so foreign. Was that because I only remember the last time I spoke with her before she died, when she was so sick? Dad was just Dad – his voice and mannerisms. Maybe I haven't really grieved my loss. Maybe I just put it away."

I thought about those pictures hanging around the pit, and the pit itself, which was like one of the circles of Hell. While I walked the circumference, I had been looking for a picture of Kristin's friend Heather Ho, although the last time I'd seen her, in Hawaii, she was a thirteen-year-old girl wearing braces and a baseball cap. Heather had worked all her life to be a baker and she had a prestigious job at Windows on the World up at the top of Tower #1. But why was I thinking of her while Maryann told me about seeing the old video? Part of me didn't want to find Heather Ho. Part of me wanted to think she wasn't there among the other victims and weather-scarred photographs. In Mexico, there is a simple handmade cross to mark every highway death. Driving, you see the crosses at hairpin turns or steep drops. But there are other, unmarked spots on this earth. The tarmac where my brother crashed his plane, the highway, on the cloverleaf outside L.A., where Cesario was shot, and a place high above the waves at Hanauma Bay.

I was standing by that table I use as a desk at the cottage. Through the window, I could see the fledglings and, behind them, unlimited green, although there was the dusty road winding up between trees. I said, "But you don't even mention your own young self, Maryann. Locked away for so much longer than you expected . . . didn't you feel any pity looking at that twenty-three-year-old girl?"

She said she hated the way she looked. She had a shoulder-length perm.

I said, "None of us likes to look at our old perms . . . but it's possible to feel some nostalgia for our innocence."

Maybe it was the wrong word to use. Maryann was quiet for a while. Then she said, "I find myself stuffing the emotions I feel."

"I know you do. The parole boards always say you show no remorse. No insight. Could you let go of that control?"

"I can't. Not in here."

"Because you might say something or get in trouble?" People listen. People report on each other.

"I guess I've learned to hold myself in check." Voice flat.

I was looking out at the road. It was empty. From the kitchen, there was the smell of chicken cooking on the stove. Garlic and soy sauce. Maryann was talking and I was remembering a dream. I'd been involved in two murders. Not committing them, but watching. Am I guilty? I wrestle with this, regretting my own paralysis – although it wasn't exactly that. It was an interested passivity. I had stood aside, aware of enormous space all around me.

38

One night in August the voice was flat again. Something was wrong, but it took a while to get there and then, because of the minutes ticking on our call, she had to do it fast. "She needed a small bit of surgery," Maryann told me, speaking about a woman she didn't name. "Went in last week. I think it was a prolapsed uterus thing or bladder. Nothing much. And she came back three days ago. We've been friends for a long time. She was here when I came in. But yesterday morning when she got out of bed she complained of chest pains. That was it. She'd been given a release date in 1983, but they kept putting it off. They gave her seven to life, not a death sentence, but that's what it was. And she was a person who was always good to everyone in here. There's such a cloud over us now – inmates and staff – everyone loved her. And she died in here."

"I'm so sorry."

"And today *Dateline* came in to do some interviews. What a time for it. We told them what happened. Then they interviewed a woman with leukemia. She had one leg amputated already and now she's had another one off. She should be gone. She's been here twenty years."

When the call came, I had just peeled my first ear of corn. All through August, we enjoy them soaked in ice water and then grilled in their husks. We'd been in the river and we were drinking a bottle of cold wine. The house was hot, but there was a little breeze coming in through the screens and the sounds of the river and birds getting settled for the night. When I answered the phone, I mentioned the corn. Then I bit my lip.

Sherrie Chapman, the inmate with cancer, had died a few months before, after being denied a compassionate release. And death must be impersonal in prison, where someone simply disappears in the night and where, by 8:30, the women were stuck inside. The brick buildings held the heat long after the sun had set. But there was a short reprieve. At 8:40, six rows of electronic buttons began to open the cell doors in rotation so the women could sign up for phone calls. At 9:00, they were locked in again – no more chance to catch a little breeze, phone conversations finished. Maryann usually relished our phone calls as a few minutes of relief.

For me, they were something else. The two people I spoke to most often on the phone that summer were an old woman and a prisoner, neither of whom I could save. When I wasn't talking to my mother or Maryann, I was cutting young trees out of the huge chunk of Canadian Shield next to the house, grabbing and pulling and chopping as if I could free up the roots. It took me years to give up all the hodgepodge of growth on this great mound of stone – raspberry stalks and birch saplings and unrecognizable stuff with roots crawling underneath – years to care enough because at the top of this rock, a huge metal cable leads up to a hydro pole and a light that interferes with the stars.

But a month or so before, when a group of our friends were here and a lot of wine and margaritas had been drunk, there was a contest with two ugly-looking slingshots to shoot out that light. Eventually someone succeeded and, for the first time in all these years, the night was really night.

But the thing about that light we shot out is that it went cold, then flickered, then somehow relit. There was nothing left – no discernible filament – but we got out the slingshots again. Would one go back in time? Would one call back the mother who danced in the kitchen or the brother who taught us to swim? We cleaned up the broken glass and lay with our backs on the rock to take a good long look at the sky. Funny to think this piece of ground is the one I've known longest in my life and Maryann's been in prison longer than I've been here.

39

That winter was going to be a tale of two cities: In Vancouver, my daughter was pregnant with twins and the pregnancy was so precarious that she was confined to bed for several months. In Topeka, my mother was dying, but not so that anyone noticed. "I've been lazy today," she'd report. "But what could be nicer than lying here reading in bed?"

I went to see her.

I went to see my daughter. I came home and paced and wondered which one I should visit next. I was frightened. At such times we want to make everything right, hold back the fates, put all the pieces together again. I was frightened, and instead of going to see my child or my mother, I went to see Maryann. Getting off the plane, I was actually not sure what I was doing there. And the only motel room I could find had to be rented from a man who stood behind bulletproof glass. There were old Band-Aids in the shower; there was no phone. But I tried to compare my room with Maryann's cell as I pulled back the unpleasant bedspread and crawled in under it.

The next morning, the prison was exactly as I had left it, even to the stout woman at the desk at the visitors' centre. Same woman. Same giant scissors. "Are you wearing an underwire bra?" Maryann had to be called away from work, but she was allowed to see me because I had come from so far away. The only other visitors were two women, elegant and well dressed. With them sat Leslie van Houten, one of the three Manson girls. "I didn't know they were in prison with you. All this time and you never told me. Do you know them? What are they like? Do they stick together? How do the other women feel about them?" Leslie was very thin, with a long braid that was grey and a look of suffering stamped into her face.

It was a warm, overcast day and the prison, surrounded by those same thousands of cows, was blanketed by the smell of their shit. The stench was so overwhelming that I almost gagged. The visiting room was hot and there were hundreds of big, buzzing flies. We pulled two plastic chairs up to a bench and sat facing each other, knee to knee, eye to eye. "Do you want to meet Leslie?"

"Yes." I'd parked my rental car next to a new Lincoln that one of the visitors must have been driving.

"That's her mother. And a friend who brings her out here." Maryann was wearing the glasses I'd had an optometrist send down from Portland. I'd carried her prescription into a shop and picked out the frames. I'd had to explain the situation, that I could not send them myself; it was against the rules. I'd asked one of the clerks to try them on because she looked a little like Maryann, if Maryann could wear bubbly hair and bright red lipstick.

When Leslie's visitors got up to leave, she came past us on her way out. In a minute she would be strip-searched. Then she would go off to her job or back to her cell, but now Maryann introduced us and Leslie gripped my hand, gazing at me with huge eyes and looking nothing like the young woman who carved an X on her forehead during her murder trial. "I've heard about you," she said.

I said I'd heard about her as well.

I was going to have two days with Maryann – days when I should have been someplace else – and I hoped there would be time to talk about things we had not talked about before. We'd talked about the progress of her writ; had she heard from Mike Brennan? We'd talked about Valere, whose parole hearing was coming up. "She might get out this time."

"That will be like a divorce," I had told Maryann.

"Death," she had said.

We'd talked about William, about her father and mother and . . . "Did you ever get mad at them?" I asked.

"Just once," she said, without stopping to think. "It was in Hawaii, during the trial. Dad had told me he had some money set aside. Money to help me if I really needed it. So one day this smooth lawyer named Winston Mirakitani finds me on a bench outside the courtroom. He's really short but flashy in a white suit and he says he can get me off for $50,000. So I call Dad and he says he doesn't have the money. That made me really mad. But that's the only time."

I was sitting in a room buzzing with flies and heat and I told myself that my mother was simply old, simply fading, simply not feeling well as she had been old and fading and not feeling well for three years. I told myself that Esta would be all right and I crossed my fingers and leaned back in my chair. I said, "He still owned the house in Phoenix, didn't he?"

Maryann shut her eyes. "But he'd told the tenants they could have it for as long as they needed."

"You needed it more. He could have sold it to save you."

"Oh, he'd never go back on his word."

My father, if thou hast opened thy mouth unto the

Lord, do to me according to that which hath proceeded out of they mouth. Judges XI. "I got the box," I said, to change the subject. "How many thousands of pages did you send?" I had wanted to compare the court testimony to the words I'd written in my yellow notebook, but when a box half the size of a bathtub arrived, I'd more or less given up. Had I actually listened to all those millions and millions of words? Both lawyers had asked William to go over the most trivial details countless times and every rehashing of events was more detailed. "He walked a little ways away from the car," William had said, describing Larry's murder. "And I told Maryann to watch him, but she indicated she could watch him from in the car. I instructed him to walk down to this little ravine. It wasn't the same place where Joe was. And I know when he walked down he's going to slip and fall. And before he gets back up the road, he won't know which way we turned." There were fifty versions of that paragraph. "I could see that he's going to slip and fall. He's not going to break his neck or nothing, but he's going to probably get scratched up."

What I noticed was how much I'd missed. I hadn't written a word about the forensics expert who testified that there were only two bullets and that Larry had been shot from behind. William had stated many times that Maryann shot Larry three times while she was looking him in the face.

Where was the third bullet?

Another thing I hadn't mentioned in my notes was Bert Bray's testimony. Maryann's father had told us about talking to William in Yuma and convincing him to turn himself in. Was I listening? Did I wonder then, as I do now, why William went to Yuma instead of staying on the bus and trying to escape?

"I didn't have anywhere to keep it when Mike sent me the box," Maryann was saying. Most of the pages were things that had been recently filed on her behalf, but there were old transcripts attached. "Did William ever drive your car?" I asked now. "In Phoenix?"

"Yes. All the time. He'd come by to see me at work and ask for money."

"And that was a VW, but he said in court that he couldn't drive a stick shift."

"He could. He did. Definitely."

"Why would he bother with that little lie?" Mike Brennan, at USC, was trying to show that the State of Hawaii had depended on the testimony of a known informant, that they had allowed him to perjure himself when he said he was serving life without parole. But maybe William lies without even realizing it. Maybe he even believes what he says. In one of his letters, William had written to Maryann, "Don't sweat it. You'll go free as I will not be believed and you will. I know this, and when

· you're out there, think of how I freed you. Think of the price you cost me."

I noticed that another prisoner had come in to meet a visitor. "He comes all the time," Maryann said, when I asked about them. I asked because they sat together like elderly couples sometimes sit, bowed over with foreheads together, as if their moments together were measured and cherished.

"How old is she?"

"In her seventies, I guess. She killed an abuser. Not hers, though. Someone else's." The woman was small and delicately built. Her husband held her hand tenderly. That evening Maryann was supposed to make a speech in front of the warden at a meeting of the Life Termers' Organization. She had recently been elected president and she took her duties seriously. Her speech would be about elderly prisoners, who cost the state an average of $66,000 a year. "There's a woman here on dialysis," she told me. "Has to go out to the hospital twice a week under guard. And do you have any idea what those guards get paid? A younger prisoner costs about $28,000 to keep. That's a big difference. It's stupid to keep old women locked up. What harm are they going to do anybody?" Then she recited the statistic for lifers, which she knows by heart. Less than 1 per cent come back once they're released. "We just don't come back. Our crimes are crimes of circumstance."

"Maryann," I said suddenly. "Let's find your birth mother."

"I told you she had me when she was sixteen?"

"Yes, you did. Yes."

"And did I tell you it was my mother who left my father and me? He gave me up, but he did it out of love and wanting what was best for me. That's why I decided I wanted to know who he was. I'd been asking my mom questions about him, but she wouldn't tell me anything. Finally I told her that no one could ever take her and dad's place in my heart or my life, and she sent me a copy of the adoption papers."

"In here?"

"Yes. Containing my birth parents' names. Hers was Anna Foster. His is Herbert Douglass. I was born Kerry Jean Douglass, which is kind of strange to think about."

"Why don't we . . ."

"I don't really have anyone left."

"You have Penne."

"Not quite."

"Anna Foster could still be alive."

"I know, but I don't care about her – especially after what my father told me. The last time he saw her was when he took her the divorce papers to sign. She was working in a bar. In Phoenix. Mother Anna." She looked away.

Included in the pages of testimony were all the things we had not been allowed to hear – the bench conferences between the judge and the attorneys and his instructions to them. Hioki kept trying to prevent things. That was his tactic, but he didn't seem to know what he was up against.

"Then what happened?"

"She shot him, shot him."

"How many times?"

"Three."

I told Maryann I would see her in the morning, and I went out slowly, with nothing to do for the rest of the night but read more pages of testimony. The parking lot was empty and when I climbed the three steps to the guesthouse to retrieve my car key, the keeper handed them over, she of the scissors. But when I put the key in the car lock, the car alarm went off and I glanced quickly up at the guard towers. There were guns trained on me.

40

Saturdays at the prison are busy. This one had the usual young fathers holding babies, and grandmothers with older children or other relatives. A father gave his infant a bottle without looking at her, then held her up on his shoulder and slapped at her back, saying, "Good girl, good girl." Another cycle, I thought.

The scissor-lady in the guesthouse had smiled at me. The day before, she had helped me call the car rental place and they had told me to use the button on my keypad instead of the key. I had not been shot or arrested and I had found a nicer place to sleep. Today we can sit outside where the flies are less pestering and where there are more things to be seen. A mother and daughter whispering to each other in Spanish. And a prisoner named Anika, who is from Sweden. "She just wants to go home, but California won't let her."

I also meet Pat, another Manson girl, who tells me she reads every book that I send Maryann. Pat's mother is visiting in a wheelchair and they sit together for several hours, two heads bent.

"How was the speech last night?"

"It went great. I was nervous having the warden right there in front of me, but he seemed impressed with my research."

The usual moment of disinclination overwhelms me. My mother. My child. Why am I here instead of there? "Maryann, in court William mentioned other robberies. He told the arresting officer in L.A. that there were several in both California and Hawaii."

"In California, yes. But not in Hawaii."

"You're sure? Why would he say that?"

"I don't know."

"Why didn't you disagree?"

"They never asked me."

"True. Hioki dropped the ball a hundred times. But why didn't they interview you in California?"

"Because," she lowers her gaze, "I wouldn't talk to them without my lawyer and he wouldn't give them anything without a deal."

"William said you did one robbery alone?" I'm looking through the new glasses and into her eyes, which are suddenly wet. "Tell me."

On June 25, while Larry Hasker's body was being found and moved and identified in Hawaii, Maryann acted as lookout while William robbed a store in Downey, California. The next day, in Bellflower, she went into a U-Totem store, pulled a gun out of her purse, threatened the clerk, and took the money in the till while William waited in Cesario Arauza's stolen car. "And that woman had a breakdown. She'd been robbed before two times and she ended up in a mental hospital." A pause. "I did that to her. I took that piece of her life. I mean, she went home again, back to her kids, but I did that. The others were different, but that one was mine . . . and why didn't I just tell her to call the cops, there was a lunatic in the car outside?"

"Did you use the gun?"

"I had it."

"Tell me about when you got picked up by Cesario Arauza. Because I have a theory. You can tell me if it makes sense."

"We started hitchhiking. To northern California," she says quietly. "I think it was the same day we landed in L.A., but I'm not sure any more. Then we were coming back down."

"So Cesario picked you up and William was sitting in back."

"We had been riding with him for several hours when William pulled the gun on him and told him to pull off to the side. The man didn't have that much money on him. I don't know what William had in his mind."

"And he was nice to you."

"Who?"

"Cesario. In his testimony, William said you stopped someplace and tried to leave without him, the two of you." The words William had used were elaborate. Like my one-horned goat. He'd said, They wanted to throw me out and keep going, and there's a lot of ramifications as to why it happened. You know, it went over and over and over and over and over. And it was a senseless thing, and it happened, you know. "He said Cesario made a pass at you. Or that's what you told him."

"We never stopped until William told him to. Then they got out and walked down an embankment and I heard the gunshots."

"Maybe he thought you were planning to go off together. The way you were going off with Larry Hasker after you dropped William at the apartment."

"But that was William's idea. That's what *he told Larry* when he asked him for a ride home."

"Because Larry was coming on to you. But Joe Leach was different. He was a lot older than William. Forty something. And he never really tried anything, did he? And those were the only three people you and William were ever alone with. Am I right? Larry Hasker and Cesario were your age. They were young. He thought they were coming on to you. Remember how William described Cesario? I just read it again in the testimony. 'He was bigger. A lot bigger.'" Surely someone in the last twenty or so years must have suggested this. Someone must have thought of jealousy as a motive.

"I never thought of that," Maryann says, although she always describes her ex-husband as possessive, controlling. "He said that he got messages, that killing Arauza was part of a plan."

"So control was a huge part of his reality."

"It was always there. I was always being tested. He'd say, What did I tell you yesterday? And I'd have to recite it."

Stand up straight. What did I tell you? What did I just say?

The night Maryann was arrested in Long Beach, William had asked her to go out and get him some cigarettes. He'd given her the car keys. He'd let her out of his sight for the first time since the Joe Leach robbery. It was her chance to escape. But minutes later she was pulled over by the police. Had he called them? When she took the police back to the motel, or when they took her, William wasn't there, but he had left her glasses case in the room and in it there were four bullets, all hollow points.

While she was taken off to jail and charged with robbery, William got himself down to Yuma. And how did Maryann's father manage not to strangle this overgrown boy? Instead, they sat in the living room drinking ginger ale and fingering paper napkins until William got up and paced back and forth in front of his father-in-law. He was wired and volatile. Hungry. His knit shirt was torn. He had come for help and eventually he let Bert call the sheriff. "But can I have some breakfast first?"

"Are you known by any other names?" the sheriff asked him.

"He had a thing about my dad," Maryann says. "He used to call him all the time from jail. Collect, you know. And when my mom answered, she'd just hang up. But Dad would take the call."

"My father used to say he would never bail me out."

"Were you ever mad at him?"

"I never got as far as that. Just scared. But I was mad at my mother once."

"My dad took those calls out of love," says Maryann proudly, and we move from that to the love so evident all around us . . . the sight of these relatives and friends, of these church mentors and penpals and strangers going through the loops, taking the time: the husband who comes week after week, year after year. The mother. The teenager in a black hooded sweatshirt, pulling the hood up around his face and then letting it down. Even the evident affection between Maryann and Anika, between Maryann and Pat. Her tone when she mentions Valere . . . "We went to dinner last night because they were serving something edible." And the story of Valere eating all the fudge Maryann had made in the immersion pot. Don't you want your cocoa and chocolate pudding too?

"What was it with your mother?" Maryann asks now.

"She told me to give up a certain boy."

Maryann is quiet. Then she laughs.

"Lucky you."

41

Now, when it is too late, I remember Maryann telling me her two regrets. The first one was William. The other one was not being with her parents when they were dying. Next to my desk there are two photographs of my mother. One, taken in her early thirties, is the face I gazed at from my crib or from my highchair or even from her lap, although I don't remember her holding me. This photograph is an enlargement that Michael and Kristin made for the funeral. They also enlarged the other one, taken at her ninetieth birthday lunch, where she is holding up an icy glass of vodka and looking bemused by all of us. We had gathered to celebrate a birthday she could not accept. We had bullied her out of her bed and up onto her feet. We had dressed her in creamy silk and put a corsage on her breast. We had come from hither and yon, from the now and the past, and we had made a party for her with all the love that she had given us. Sometimes I look at the second picture and sometimes at the first. They are both my mother. Since her death, I seem to have fallen in love with her along with my brand-new granddaughter, as if I am a link between what is gone and what is to come. How not to think of the boy who unzipped his pants at the beach? Or the woman in prison. Unwanted babies and babies who represent life.

By the time we got to Topeka, my mother was lying on a steel table in the storage room of a funeral home. She was cold, having been in a freezer. I had told them not to touch her. I did not want her embalmed.

Kristin and I went in with a paper bag. Is all grief more or less the same? Ask Mr. and Mrs. Hasker, who did not have the satisfaction of a finished life. Ask Maryann, who lives on both ends of it. The bag held a silk dress, a pair of stockings, earrings, and the Fabergé egg she liked to wear on a chain.

Someone closed the door behind us.

Mother was naked, covered with a sheet. Her hair had been washed a few days before, but had lost its set. Falling back from her face as she lay on that table, it was longer than usual, and her beautiful nose was more hooked, the nostrils open and dark. Her mouth was drawn back. Here was flesh pared down as if carved by a careful knife.

Mother used to say, "I don't know who will see me dead. I worry about this." But as Kristin and I combed her hair and washed her face and thought about what underwear she would want – all of it? – but that was so much, too much – we both cried as we talked to her. A ruby red slip. Panties. Stockings: the old-fashioned kind in two separate pieces. (We had found a pair ready, in her bureau. Who put them there? She always wore the other kind.) A touch of lipstick. Her silver earrings. So that here is my mother stretched out in her purple dress and when I am alone with her I can climb on the table and bury my face in her breast as I never could do in her air-breathing life. I can open her lips to pour her last pleasure of vodka between them. I can open her eyes and rub my tears into them, flakes of anger washed away.

I know she will do as she has always done: wait for my father, who is late, for my brother, who is gone, for her comforts, which are private, and her long death, which is begun.

Because of the funeral, I was late getting to Vancouver but I arrived a few hours before the twins were born. Two months early. The littlest one did not survive.

As a family, we are shaken to the bones. Have known death and birth and death. Have grieved and rejoiced and grieved.

Sometimes now, I lie half-awake for fifteen or twenty minutes in the morning, having dreamed that I am not in a coffin but in prison. Worrying up the details. That watching of clocks. On the one hand, time stretches out like those railroad tracks in pictures that describe infinity. But the other clock, the one that lives in our bodies, ticks faster and faster. I am going to die and never get out. I imagine that as an old woman I'll take to my bed and live like this, in the half-light, exactly as my mother did at the end. "There may come a day," she would say, "when I just refuse to get up. Like the old aunt did in Proust."

Only when a nurse forced her into the shower and down to the hairdresser did she decide she had really had enough.

Of course I am grateful to this nurse, as I am grateful to every single one of the good people who took care of my mother over the last two years of her life. Would that I had done it all! I felt so heroic, so necessary when I flew into Kansas City, rented a car, drove to Topeka, and stumbled into my mother's apartment – the place I had foisted on her. Usually, I found her in bed. Usually it was time for lunch. "You're not dressed!" I'd bark at her, before we had managed our usual furtive kiss.

"Oh well, I thought you'd have eaten. I didn't know what time you'd be here."

"But you! It's lunchtime for you. I could smell the food downstairs when I came in."

"Oh well. I've had something."

"Such as what?" I actually liked the food downstairs. For some idiotic reason, eating in this dining room always cheered me up. It made me feel young, vital, and compassionate. I took an interest in each old face, each trembling conversation. I leaned into the space between the tables the better to eavesdrop. There were moments when I wanted to embrace every resident. I loved the staff. Once, when Kristin and I were visiting together, we asked for a meeting with them to discuss Mother's lethargy. Mother came to the meeting with us. We said we were becoming really worried. She had given up on the exercise class in the morning and there was the new tendency not to eat. They had turned off her stove after she sent billows of smoke down the hall. That was awful, like having to give up her car. She had a toaster oven, but she kept trying to make toast on the heating pad of the coffee pot. She cooked her eggs in the water as it slowly heated up. What should we do?

The director told Mother that she should come to the exercise class. "Oh my," said Mother coyly. "I had no idea. Why of course I'll come. What time is it, did you say?" She had always complained about the early hour of this class, but now she smiled and said, "Fine. Fine," and I knew that she was really done. She had defended my father, dead now for thirty years. She had been stylish and witty and charming and smart. She had kept her chin up when my brother's death had mangled her heart. She had learned to speak Spanish; she liked to conjugate. She had made elegant meals. She had knit and embroidered and sewn and created exquisite decoupaged boxes and eggs. She had entertained the Ballet Russe and made light of my obvious failings. She had taken care of me, of my cats and dogs and fish. With her bare hands. Even when they were arthritic. She had said, When you feel envy and wish you were someone else, remember that you have to take the whole life.

My mother was my age when she became a widow. Then she survived for another thirty-three years. And thirty-three is a good number. In that time she learned to manage her own small pension and the few stocks left to her. She sold the big house and moved into a tiny one two blocks away and seemed not to look back, although she dreamed, she said, only of the larger house, the place she had created in her prime. Because she lived those thirty-three years so very well, I have my map to a good old age. Yes, I see it coming and it cannot frighten me. I feel her legs in my legs, her back in my back. I go to the kitchen to make coffee and remember that she always readied hers before she went to bed. Soon I will do the same. We do not practise age. It is performed for us. We see the lines and movements in our elders. In our retrieval of those things, we capture the people we have loved. Contain them once they are lost.

42

Maybe I liked flying down to Corona, jumping in a rented car, and arriving at the prison with my good cheer and health intact the way I liked flying down to my mother when she was still within reach. Maybe I liked knowing that neither Mother nor Maryann could get up and follow me. I was in charge.

When Maryann describes her life, she talks about the jobs she's held and her two-year college degree. Her accomplishments feel as real to her as mine do to me. She sent me a basket she'd made out of pine needles, although acquiring the materials takes weeks. She reads books on tape for blind students. She belongs to organizations that manage to do things for people outside. So, when she learned that her sister had cancer, she was stunned, then hurt, then angry; she felt cut off and betrayed. Penne had known for three years. She'd been through three surgeries, chemo-therapy, and the usual dose of fear, but Maryann had never been told. "It was along the lines of finding out I had a great-nephew when he was three years old," Maryann wrote to me. "It's like I don't count as close-enough family to share these little tidbits with." When the anger passed, she thought about Penne being the last of her family. She had not let Maryann call her for several years, saying it ran up her phone bill, but she had been out there – someone in the world who knew Maryann from the very begin-ning. "I wonder if I'll make it out of here in time to see her and spend some time with her. Even though we haven't been the closest of sisters, I don't like the thought of losing my whole family while I'm in here!"

It was impossible to write back to her dying sister. At the time of their parents' fiftieth wedding anniversary, Maryann had asked her father on the phone if anyone was going to throw a party. He had sounded rueful. "No one to do that but Penne," he'd said. "And you and I know that's doubtful." Maryann had contacted Penne and sug-gested that they do something to mark the event. "I can't do much in here," she had written, "but I saw a cross-stitch sampler I'd like to do and maybe you could help." At that point Penne had rallied. And in 1992, when she read about William's confession in *California Legal Magazine*, it was Penne who contacted Deborah Fraser about the confession and then helped Fraser worry up legal and historical details. This was something; this was almost good. But when Gladys got sick, Penne abandoned Maryann. "She said there was a bank account with my name on it and that she was in charge of it. I guess she'd always been jealous of me in a lot of ways," Maryann says. "My logical mind says she didn't tell me about her cancer because she didn't want me to worry. . . . But another part wants to let her know how I felt like she still doesn't accept me as her sister and that I just really don't matter to her."

"But she sent your father's letter."

"Long after the fact and reluctantly. And the will. I've never seen it. I don't know what's in the bank account. Maybe nothing. She won't tell me."

I told her about my mother's brown suitcase. How she had been proud of it – stylish and round with a long, looped strap. I said she had used it, over the last years of her life, to store a collection of letters my father had written to her during the war. Once, I had asked if I could read them. He was my father. I had no similar pile of letters from him, not even one letter to keep in a private drawer. My mother had made a sound. They were sent to her, she'd told me flatly. Her alone. What's more, she'd taken scissors to them so I would never read certain words.

Scissors.

I promised myself that I would read what was left of those wartime letters the minute my mother died. When she moved to the shiny new apartment, I shoved the round suitcase under her bed and tapped it with a hand or a foot whenever I came to see her. On each visit, I slid it an inch or two farther under the bed so she would not notice it. The day would come, I told myself, when it would not matter if I opened the suitcase and read those letters. But when I had her belongings sent up to Toronto after her death, there was no brown suitcase among the boxes. I've been through the papers, the books, the photographs. I've wanted to learn how he spoke to her, how he thought about things, how he expressed himself when he was different.

There must have been such a time.

But she kept his secrets, even as she lay dying.

A few weeks later, when Maryann called to tell me Penne was dead, I couldn't believe it. Then I realized Penne had never been real. Not to me. After all our letters and conversations, I still didn't believe that Maryann had a life or a story beyond the walls of the prison. Oh dear God, I said, and I meant it, because Maryann would never have a chance to make things right with Penne now. This sister who refused her phone calls. This sister who sent her a form letter explaining her terminal disease. This sister who had better things to do than visit an inmate. "Will you send flowers for me?" the inmate asked. "There's no way to do it from in here."

43

Of course summer, as usual, followed that wild spring. We went back up to the cottage as we have always done. When I got phone calls from Maryann, I didn't remind her that our correspondence had been going on for three years, that this was a kind of anniversary, that three years before, her attorney was about to reopen her case. He had filed a writ. Delays and more delays. Postponements. I didn't tell her that I should have gone to Topeka instead of Corona, that I will regret that decision for the rest of my life.

She told me she'd dreamed that she called home to talk to her father and Governor Davis answered the phone. Maryann asked him why he wouldn't let anyone out of prison when so many women deserved to be released. And how could he visit her father and yet deny him the chance to spend his last years with her?

I told her I'd called Larry Hasker's father. "I said I might want to write about the murder and about your case and would he tell me about Larry. I wanted to know about his childhood, about his personality, about his hopes and dreams because it seems wrong to leave him out of your story."

For a few seconds, Maryann didn't say anything. Then she said, "What happened?"

"With Mr. Hasker? Well, he didn't want to talk to me about Larry if I was writing a book about you." Then I said I had tried to find Kimberly, Larry's sister. In the courtroom she was just a girl, a sister, someone who had been called to testify. But later, in my mind, she became a person with unbearable grief. That was after I knew what it was to lose a brother, although it was a grief I could never describe. A brother is a piece of your flesh. Arm. Leg. The very same consciousness. A brother is your image in the mirror and his death is your suicide.

I said, "Kimberly seems to have disappeared."

Maryann said she was hot and I told her that I was about to jump in the river. Why protect her from the truth of my life? My hands were dirty. I'd been planting a star-gazer lily in a place where it will stand out and be noticed. I told her I had visions of a more civilized landscape – a bush here, a clump of flowers there. I had a brand-new granddaughter to think about. Since her birth and my mother's death, I could see my life played out on this land-scape. But what does a person do without such a set of rocks and trees, board and roof? I was still reading through the pages Maryann had sent – bits and pieces of old testimony. They included the actual plea agreement William had signed with Charles Marsland. And Jan Futa's name was there as well. Another set of papers in the box involved jailhouse informants. In 1988, the L.A. district attorney announced that no more jailhouse informants were to be used as witnesses. But William was gone by then, of course, practising his trade in other states.

When I drove off to our little town with its one clothing store, one drugstore, one grocery store, it was because Maryann had asked me to send her a quarterly box. Sheron was sick and there was no one else, so I told Maryann it would be a pleasure to send the thirty pounds of candy and nuts and dried tuna and tea and coffee she was allowed to receive, although the denim shorts she needed were required to have an eleven-inch inseam and they might be hard to find.

In California, there was about to be a recall of Governor Davis. This was not because he had never, in all his years in office, paroled a prisoner with a life sentence. Instead, he was accused of abusing state funds. In Texas, the democrats had gone into hiding in order to prevent a vote that would redistribute legislative districts and thereby give Republicans a decisive majority in Congress. In Hawaii, there was going to be a conference call with Maryann's lawyer. Would Jan Futa have done what she was supposed to have done?

At the prison, the warden had invited a few people from a program called Canine Service Training in for a tour. Not only did they come, inspecting cells, yards, and prisoners, they also brought four dogs along with them. The dogs were trained to help people with disabilities. Some of the trainers were nuns. The morning of the tour, Maryann had gone to work and someone mentioned the visiting dogs. Maryann looked at her boss, who said, "Oh, go on!" and she found the dogs in front of her housing unit along with their trainers, the warden, several administrators, and a number of lifers, who hadn't been close to a dog in twenty or thirty years. The nuns were allowing them to pet the dogs and some of the women were crying. All of this had an impact on the warden, who decided that CIW should participate in the program.

"You love animals," I said.

Maryann said, "But what if I get called out to court in Hawaii?"

I teased her about not being able to commit when she was serving a life sentence. I said it was the way her father had been when he came home from the war. Paralyzed. I said, "If you get called, you'll go. You have to let them see you. Represent yourself. But you should do the dogs."

She answered quickly. "If I go out of here, even for a night, I lose my room. I lose my roommate and my neighbours in the unit. If I don't have to go, I won't."

That summer, along with phone calls from Maryann, I had an invitation from my old Topeka girlfriends, who were going to get together for several days on a lake in Minnesota. It would be our first glimpse of each other in forty years, since none of them had come to the high-school reunion. Most of us had gone to nursery school together. We had lived within a few blocks of each other. Our mothers were our Scout leaders and had something called the Mothers' Group while, among the daughters, relationships varied in intensity over the years. All through grade school I was closest to Joyce, who lost her hearing in the fifth grade. Would she mind me telling this? No, it is one of the things that has defined her life. Another is her Jewish family, therefore her difference from the rest of us. I thought it was exciting that they had no Christmas tree, that the four daughters received gifts for eight consecutive nights. I thought it was miraculous that she learned to read lips so I could talk to her silently from across the room.

In high school, I was closest to Wendy, who lived in the house behind mine. We shared double dates with two boys who were best friends. The car, the drive-in movies, the path between our houses, the phone every night. Joyce, Wendy, and the rest of them would be together in Minnesota and the thought of it terrified me. The rest of them had kept in contact. The rest of them had seen each here or there or somewhere between. The rest of them knew about husbands and children and parents. Who had been born, who had died. These childhood friends would still be married to original husbands. Would have lived normal lives. They had never burned bridges. What did we now have in common? We had known each other's parents: the mothers who stayed home except when they went to the beauty shop or the grocery store; the fathers who drove off in new model American cars every morning and who were each and every one Republican to the core except for mine, who stood out with his old car, his liberal views, and his returns from the office at midnight. I wondered how Maryann would feel about meeting old friends again. For three years, I'd wanted to go back with her to Honolulu. I had pictured her there, running down those courthouse steps, as if all the stories I'd read and all the movies I'd seen and all the TV shows I'd watched were promises of what could really happen. It had seemed significant that her lawyer decided to reopen the Hawaii case the week I first wrote to her – as if something was pulling us together.

I found a pair of denim shorts in our country store. I had brought a tape measure. I tried to forget about Mr. Hasker, his bitterness, his ache. And Kimberly. For an entire week, the quarterly box and the invitation kept my mind elsewhere.

44

"Why didn't you ever answer my letters?" Wendy asked. "Didn't you know that I loved you?"

"After Mexico," said Joyce, "I never saw you again. We were so close. I was closer to you than to anyone else in my life."

I did my best to explain, but I noticed that much of the time I spent with my childhood friends in Minnesota was concerned with our mothers.

All being dead except three.

Liz's mother, in fact, drove over to see us and stayed for a glass of champagne. She was alert, interested in each of us, and stimulating. Sitting gracefully in her chair with her ankles crossed, wearing stockings and small heels, wearing jewellery that suited her and attractive clothes – pants and a silk shirt – she made me ache. We all felt the same. We hovered around Liz's mother and drank in her intelligence, her questions and opinions. Mulled wine, she was, to our motherless bodies.

So here we are, tending our mothers in memory or in the flesh, my own most intimate moments with my mother being after her death. I cannot really tell my friends about this, although without those minutes in the basement of the funeral home, I would never have recognized my terrible need. Instead, we talk about living mothers, the ones that are left. We talk about their depressions, their housing, the long curled toenails on arthritic feet. How much are we willing to give of ourselves to our parents? How angry or selfish are we? How much do we still resent the old brutalities and withheld faith? Someone says that being a grandmother will change me. I will give up my investment in judging. I will finally see another person uncritically.

It's odd, but we are not much interested in our children during these magical four days. What we have in common is our own childhoods and the secrets we never shared back then and the secrets we didn't even know we had. Because we grew up in Topeka, we talk about the famous court case that bears its name and what it meant to them and to me. *Brown vs. The Board of Education of Topeka.* It was the fiftieth anniversary of the Supreme Court decision that summer, and we had been hearing about it in the news. SCHOOL SEGREGATION BANNED, the headlines had read back in 1953. And now, sitting on folding chairs by a Minnesota lake, someone says, "But in fifth grade we already had Alice and Fanny in our school."

I say that was because my father was president of the schoolboard. How could they not have realized? And suddenly I'm thinking, what a father. He ran for the schoolboard because I couldn't spell. He ran because he wanted to restore the teaching of phonics to our schools. He wanted the best public education possible for me. For everyone. Then he got embroiled in schoolboard politics. He wanted teachers to be promoted according to merit and that enraged the teachers' union. Most of the teachers turned against him. They were about to build a school on a floodplain that belonged to someone powerful and rich – another dangerous enemy. My father stopped the contract. There were threats, a lawsuit. It was a scandal. And when the Browns sued the schoolboard because their daughter was refused admission to a certain public school, my father said the Browns were right. Schools that were separate facilities could not, by definition, be equal. And equality of opportunity is what the U.S. Constitution guaranteed.

As a ten-year-old, I had no idea that the Supreme Court decision was going to change the world. What I knew was that my father was never home, was always at meetings, was more and more volatile. He was losing friends and clients. There were stores we didn't enter, people my parents wouldn't see. There were children I didn't play with any more. Teachers who didn't seem to like me. I kept getting in fights and being sent to the principal's office.

If Topeka decided to integrate the schools, as my father wished, should the board still defend itself at the Supreme Court or should it drop out of the case? For the first time, schoolboard meetings were open to the public. My father wanted the town to decide for itself. But he wanted the Supreme Court to establish a precedent. He wanted the case to be heard and won by the Browns and he wanted Topeka to be a model for everyone else. It was an odd fence to straddle, but he managed to straddle it, starting the process of desegregation with my classroom on the privileged side of town, so there would be less argument. Linda Brown's school would have to wait.

Often, I heard him shouting into the phone. I heard him get up in the middle of the night. He had a workbench in the garage, and he'd go out there and work on the sailboat, although he never managed, after that year, to put it back in the lake. In the morning, he would rush off to his law practice, but he grew more and more exhausted, more and more short-tempered, and I began to run when I saw him coming.

Up to the bathroom again, where I locked the door.

But now, telling the story to my friends, it began to make sense.

That long ago year, I had two best friends. Joyce was one of them and Alice Smith was the other. Alice was accomplished in all sorts of ways that were new to me. She hit homeruns at recess and rode her bike without touching the handlebars. She was full of jokes and good at arithmetic. I'd never known a black person before, except for our cleaning lady, but Alice was convincing proof that ability had nothing to do with race. Secretly, I felt a certain pride in her accomplishments, knowing that my father had given Alice to our school.

Looking back on it from this distance, my father seems to have struggled for something that would have happened anyway, but maybe there is more to it than that. In a pile of papers in Mother's house I found the old news clippings about *Brown vs. The Board* and read enough to understand the part my father played in an important part of history. He was thirty-nine years old when he was elected to the schoolboard and he died sixteen years after Linda Brown won her case. But what my father did was deliver a cogent argument against segregation and helped Topeka do what was right before it was ordered to do it. While he was at it, he gave the Browns room to win their case.

The news clippings were part of a mess of papers I found in my mother's house when I was going through everything after she died. I also found the single-spaced instruction sheet I was given before the mock trial about the goat – the trial I had a role in at the law school as a witness, knees together and back straight. At the bottom of the first page it says: *Return this script to the Dean's office after the trial,* as if it is to be held in strictest confidence. And something else. In the mess of papers there was a fat manila envelope. Hard to believe, but finding the old newsclippings and the goat story and a fat envelope was as important to my growing sense of understanding as talking to Maryann or sitting with childhood friends beside a Minnesota lake.

As it turns out, the injured party in the mock trial was not a goat but a little boy. The boy's arm was broken. There was a car involved and a goat too, but the goat was unharmed. Not so my father. The manila envelope was full of letters from various doctors and certain close friends and associates. They were written to the Internal Revenue Service because my father had not paid his taxes for several years. Many years. Each of the letters said, in one way or another, that my father's mental health during the decade before his death was deteriorating. Along with his friends, medical professionals testified – doctors and psychiatrists –

that my father was clinically depressed. They put the start of his condition at about the time of the Topeka tornado in 1966, when a company he had invested in was badly hit. He had put all our money into this business, trying to save it for one of his clients. He had put other peoples' money in as well, although he should not have done that. Without enough insurance, the damage should have meant the end, but my father took out further loans and cashed in his life insurance and mortgaged our house. He did not want the men at the plant to be out of work. He could not lose the money he'd put into the company or the money he had borrowed from other clients. Who knows what else was at stake? The letters were written after his death because my mother had been left nearly penniless and the IRS was going to make her pay.

I probably shook my head, sitting there on the floor reading those letters, because I knew that the condition they described had started much earlier – years before the tornado in 1966. "Spell *precipitous*," he'd snap his fingers. "Now! And look at me. Stand up straight. What did I say? Answer me." This temper, this lack of patience, this chronic irritability came home with my father from the war, that's what I think, the way Bert's indecision and paralysis came home with him. My guess is that when my father got out of the Studebaker that day in 1945 and was told that he'd have to get the ladder out of the garage and climb up to the second-floor bathroom window to see his two-year-old daughter, he felt the first prickling of rage. He had come from the train station, where my mother had gone to pick him up. He had climbed out of the car and, because of the injury to his back, because of jumping down to the ground from that troop plane in Honolulu and then reaching up to catch his bag, he must have limped as he walked up the driveway. I can see my brother running out of the house and grabbing his father around the waist, so happy to see him after that long year away. He's been watching from the front-room window or even crouching by the bushes outside. "Linda's locked herself in the bathroom," he says, and my father, who would never again sleep painlessly through a night, had to fetch the ladder and lean it against the side of the house he had tried to defend with his life.

45

There is also this. I'm in the backseat of my father's car with Joyce. He's put his favourite hat on the seat and told us not to touch it, but we are suffering from excitement, driving to Kansas City to see the Ice Capades. We are jumping around, pinching and tickling and laughing and the outcome is clear. I see us pulling up at the curb in front of my grandmother's house to bring her along with us. I see us still giggling as my father opens our door and spies his hat. We notice it too, squashed, beyond repair, beyond ever wearing again, and I know this will be the end of everything – the wonderful Ice Capades, the dinner out, the sleepover at my grandmother's house. Even in front of Joyce who, of all my friends, is my father's favourite, the happiness we've brought with us from Topeka will collapse. All the silliness disappears. We watch him brush off the hat, push at its crown, look at us for a moment, and smile.

"I used to go to the Ice Capades," Maryann says when I tell her this story. And then I decide to go see her again and this time meet Valere. Because how can I know Maryann unless I know the cellmate who probably knows her better than she knows herself? Friends are like that. They give us context. And I will have to come with a friend of my own, because only one prisoner is allowed per visitor. Susie lives in northern California and she agrees to apply for approval to visit the prison as long as we can make the entire trip in one day. She has animals to look after. So we fly.

Down south the cows are sadder than ever, but the day is cool and where there is grass, it's green. Susie can see the guard tower looming over the vast herds and I tell her there are sixteen hundred women on the human side of the fence. Having a companion along offers me a new set of eyes. I can see that those of us who are waiting outside the prison look exactly like any group clustered anyplace. We are quiet. We are variously dressed. What is unusual is our patience. The grandparents with youngsters never flinch at the flies or dust. When we get inside, we can see the people that are already lucky enough to have been reunited behind the glass. They're sitting in clusters and visiting the vending machines and by 4:00 pm, we're beginning to make jokes about the empty slots that will be left for us. "Yesterday they refilled them," someone says.

There is a slight sense of collegiality, but it is slight.

What we can see through the soundproof glass is only a tiny percentage of the two million Americans who live in prisons but, even so, Susie is astonished. "It's not even two million," I tell her. "It's more than that. Since I started writing to Maryann, another two hundred thousand people have been sent to jails. She more or less keeps me up to date." I tell Susie that her state built San Quentin first, and then, in the next hundred years, only eight more prisons got built. But during the five short years Ronald Reagan was president, nine big prisons were built. So much damage. So much harm. The death penalty was resumed. Then twelve more prisons were built. One person out of every one hundred and thirty-eight lives in one of them. "It's a business," I say. "Not just in California but all over the States. Some are privately owned. They turn a huge profit. The corporations that own them lobby for longer sentences and tighter laws because they make money off of every inmate."

"How?"

"Contracts. They're paid by the head. Like cows."

In the outside waiting area, three people are talking about the need for stricter and longer punishment. "They're someone's family?" Susie sounds horrified. But by the time we meet Maryann and Valere, we have set politics aside. We are just four women getting our food, warming it up in the microwave, making the kind of small talk any four women might make. Rain has begun outside, so we bring in the last four available plastic chairs, dry them off and sit. I'm happy to see Maryann. I no longer have to remind myself that I am the reason she is here. She is someone to whom I owe something, but there is a feeling in the room brought on by the outside rain, by the long wait, by the reunited families. And as a foursome we seem to be able to say anything. "Tell us about the strip searches. Who does them? The wardens?" Susie points to a woman in uniform with the usual weapons around her middle.

"Those are COs. The old ones were okay. But now because of Schwarzenegger they all want to retire and the new batch is overtrained. They're always just itching for something to happen."

"For what kind of things?"

"Fights," Valere says. "Yesterday they used pepper spray."

Maryann says, "It gives them a chance to strip-search us again, look for scratches or something with their flashlights."

"Do you believe her?" Susie had asked me on the plane. "I mean, is she innocent?" I had said how could I ever know. It was my usual defence. "What do we really know about anyone?" Normally, any four women I'd be chatting with over tacos and burritos might discuss a thing like strip searches done to women in prison, but normally none of us would have experienced it. On the other hand, if Valere and Maryann share our outrage, they've learned to live with it. It might be bravery or it might be something different, something I know no name for yet. Valere says Maryann is most notable for this, since she's served twenty-three years for two murders she didn't do. "I took a life," she says. "I deserved to do time."

"But why do you think so? What about the battered woman argument? Maryann says he beat you up all the time."

"I killed someone. I was doing drugs at the time. I probably wouldn't have done it otherwise."

"You didn't set out to kill him," Maryann puts in. "And he was one mean son of a bitch."

We laugh. Susie is dying to ask, so I do it for her.

Maryann says, "She shot him to stop him from hurting her. Then she ran to the backyard and hid in the dog house while he drove off."

"And then what?"

Valere sniffs, "He drove around the block."

Maryann says, "And died."

"Where did you shoot him?" Susie manages.

"Through both lungs and the heart." Valere is small and fine-featured. She wears her grey hair in a short cut and looks athletic in prison clothes. I liked her. Susie liked her. Anyone would. At this point in time, she's served eighteen years. "I'm lucky to have been here," she actually says. "It's given me time to look at myself and figure out what went wrong." She says when she gets out she won't have much life left. "My people die early. I might make it to sixty-five." Her eyes seem very large, very open wide.

It's hard to explain the intensity of these visits. They're like nothing else. Absorb and absorb and absorb. A new baby being brought to his mother. The mother in her prison garb reaching out for him. The waiting room, where we become like hostages, held in another kind of cell. We can't leave. We can't get out. We wait and watch each other and in little bits and pieces we have one two three more reasons for our hearts to break. Alone, it is almost more than I can bear. With Susie, I can enjoy seeing Maryann teased by her roommate when she doesn't speak up about her life. "Oh go on, Maryann, say it like it is. You're always so repressed!" Inmate Day Labor has been closed for a while and Maryann is working as a clerk in the mental ward. "It's peaceful," she says, although one woman hears voices that tell her to throw her lunch away and another woman believes she's being followed so she sits in the office with Maryann and cries. The mental patients don't mix with the other prisoners. Life on the yard would be too hard for them, according to Maryann. "We have to get jobs. We have to take care of ourselves! There are rules. A lot of stress." Even in prison there are prisons.

And what about the little cat, Nermal?

Maryann says he is locked up in Sheron's bathroom, where he has been since he was taken away by her. The bathroom was supposed to be a temporary arrangement, but he has been kept in there for one reason or another. A window needs to be fixed. Or it's the heating or the air conditioning or the other cats. It begins to seem that Nermal exchanged a large prison for a much smaller one. Night. Stars through a window. A lock on the door. To Maryann, it is too familiar and she doesn't want to talk about it. Finally, though, after a lot of thought, after months of deliberating, she and Valere have signed on as support providers in the puppy program, which means they have one or another dog with them for part of each day. "It's fabulous!" There will be letters and phone calls now full of news about the dogs, especially about a Golden Retriever named Jesse. "I think I'm in love," Maryann says. "And this time he's worth it."

I tell her that I talk to her lawyer every few weeks. "He sounds good. Really smart. He basically thinks Stephen Hioki did everything he had to do. I mean, *had* to do. But he also says Hioki should have investigated William for himself and not depended on the state to provide him with his information. That was crucial. The other thing he says is that Hioki should have fought harder for a deal. For you. He should have gone to the prosecutors and said, Hey look, your boy took a lie detector test and failed it and we'd like to give one to our client and make a deal for her." I decide not to tell her something else Mike Brennan had said, which was that Maryann had been in "a weird space" when she was arrested. "I don't know if this was still happening in Hawaii, but in California she was, you know, in contact with William for quite a while after she was arrested and she wouldn't co-operate in any deal against him."

I said to him, "It's called love."

I say to Maryann, "You never told me he failed a lie detector test."

Maryann says, "I forgot."

"I've got a friend in Hawaii helping me do some research," I announce. "You know, one thing's interesting. In 1982, Charles Marsland was DA. He ran on a law-and-order campaign, lock up the criminals and throw away the key because his nineteen-year-old son had been murdered on Waimanalo Beach back in 1975. He was working at Infinity Disco in Waikiki and Marsland thought he'd heard something that got him killed, got him dragged off at 4:30 in the morning and shot in the head at the beach.

Maybe he thought Larry Hasker was killed by the same gang. I think Jan Futa was under orders to get a conviction or lose her job."

Valere's nodding, as if she's sure Maryann was framed, but Maryann shrugs and smiles at a woman who killed her mother and refuses to see her children or grandchildren, refuses to ask for parole because she doesn't want to be a burden to them. It was a mercy killing, but there you are. And there is the young mother who is cuddling the baby and then stands up when the COs announce a car in the parking lot with its lights on. "I'll go fix it!" she volunteers and everyone, all of us in the visiting room, are able to laugh as one big happy-for-a-moment family. For a moment or longer, we are joined by this horrible joke. In fact, there is a good deal of joy all around, even as I see a woman circling the room with her husband, circling, circling, as if they are both trapped on one of those wheels that rodents have in their cages. Even if, outside, the rain pours down and only some of us will be leaving at eight o'clock.

Later, in the darkness of the airport parking lot, Susie closes her eyes for a minute. "I want to thank you for bringing me down here," she says. "I feel blessed by those two women."

I say I think I know what she means.

"What happened to William? What did he get out of it?"

"Mike Brennan says he didn't get much. If he'd been really smart he'd have had an attorney for the Arauza case instead of trying to do it himself. He'd have had someone who could make a really good deal for him. He'd already testified in twelve cases and they owed him big-time. But Brennan says William was still stupid back then. Meaning maybe he's not any more. Anyway, he got nothing for all his testimonies except being moved out of California and having some tattoos removed that made him look like he was in the Paramount gang, which he never was. Paramount is where he's from, and Brennan says these guys go into prison and they get tattoos to make them look like they're protected. Then they get moved to another prison where that's the wrong gang. So that's what he got for betraying the girl he married. He got his tattoos taken off."

Susie says tiredly, "And so forth." Having lived in California all her life, this is a piece of it she's never seen. Then she asks, "Is Brennan any good?"

"He filed a Writ of *Habeas Corpus* the same week I first wrote to her. I thought something would happen. It's maddening. I don't know how she can stand all the waiting. Also she can't call him because of something about the USC phone system. So she never knows what's going on. So she calls me after I call him."

"She's amazing," Susie says.

"I'm starting to think everyone should have a prisoner," I tell her.

A few days later. I tell Maryann on the phone how tired we were. How we sat in the airport parking lot trying to remember all the things we'd talked about and how we had finally just climbed out of the car and onto the plane. Maryann laughs. "Oh it's the same thing in here. We're always completely wiped out after a visiting day. You want to go straight to bed and put your head under the pillow." She says, "But don't ever think it doesn't mean a lot to us. Did I ever tell you about the time Doug – my biological – and his wife came to see me for a seventy-two-hour visit? They brought one of their kids, Shawn, and it was great, really, but I was so nervous going into it. I'd met them all before, but seventy-two hours is a long time. And do you know what?" she sounds almost childlike as the words tumble out. "I had gone through so much with Mom and finally she'd given me the adoption papers and then when I set up the visit I was worried about telling them. But Mom said, 'Well maybe we'll come on down there,' which was crazy, but the visit with Doug and Pat and Shawn was Monday through Thursday and Thursday was a normal visiting day back then. And my parents did come and it was wonderful. Maybe one of the best days of my life. Can you imagine how extremely wrung out I was afterward?

They were all here together and we spent hours like that just laughing and thanking each other. Even in a place like this you can have good memories." She adds that Doug has had a stroke and can no longer visit or speak on the phone.

46

Then I called Joe Leach. It was easy enough to find him on the Internet. He was living in California, not too many miles from Maryann. I said I was on the jury in the Maryann Acker murder trial and for a minute he didn't know what I was talking about. Then he said, Oh, it was so long ago. He said he'd seen an article in the *L.A. Times* a few years ago, but he didn't really think about it any more. The article was about L.A. County's jailhouse informant scandal and William was featured prominently.

"She's still in prison," I said.

And he said, "Well, I hope so."

It wasn't what I expected after reading his testimony. On the stand he had said, "I couldn't tell what she was feeling inside," and I had taken that for a sign that he realized she might have been acting under duress, might have been scared, might have been stupid or passive. On the stand, he portrayed William as wild and unpredictable and frightening. I'd assumed that the prosecutor had not asked further questions because she did not want to expose his doubts and I'd assumed that Hioki was not doing a good job of cross-examining.

It's possible that the years have hardened Joe Leach.

It's possible that I don't want to know what he would have said if they'd let him say it. His captors had taken his camera and pawned it. But when the L.A. police confiscated William's small bag, it had a roll of film inside with twenty-four photographs taken with Maryann's Christmas Instamatic. What were they? I can only guess. A child playing with an inflatable tube on a beach. A row of palm trees reaching like toothpicks for the sky. A slim girl wearing a blue bikini holding her hands in front of her face as if to ward off the painfulness of a flash. Where are the photographs? I ask Maryann, and she says she has no idea. "They were confiscated." I imagine a picture of William. He's standing in the Western store at Ala Moana, trying on a hat. It's a Stetson, very dark, and he's smiling under it. He's wearing jeans and a cream-coloured button-down shirt. His hair, under the hat, is brown and slightly wavy. He has sideburns, black shoes, and the look of a desert creature caught in strong headlights. The rest of the pictures? There are three of them, all blurry, of a mongoose standing up on his hind feet. "Oh look, he's posing for us," Maryann had chirped on the night they had stayed in a cave at the bay.

William must have had good memories of this place where he'd come with his other wife and her child, where he'd felt normal for two or three hours as he put on a mask and went out in the ocean to look at the fish. He didn't know how to swim, but he managed to move around in the water, holding on to the reef. You have to be raised to swim and he was the farthest thing from raised that way. What he had was smarts. What he had was his shitty life, but he'd survived and now he was back here where he'd dreamed about with a new wife and things were working out or they eventually would when he got past the emotional side of his feelings about what happened during the private hours of his life. So when they close up the park maybe they'd just stick around since there was no reason to go anyplace except maybe to eat and sooner or later they'd have to get some cash one way or another. It was private out here between the water and the hills and whatever happens won't be no big deal to nobody.

Not Joe Leach. Not Larry Hasker, who is sitting in the Garden Bar two weeks later at the Hilton Hawaiian Village. He's looking for someone called Red when he notices a man with a certain look. It takes a good eye to see this look and Larry has a good eye. "See a guy with a red beard come through here?" he asks William. It's a starter. But William doesn't bite. He's sitting alone on a bench outside the bar on the open lanai.

Hasker enters the bar. It's after ten and Red's late, or maybe Red doesn't exist. Maybe it is all a way to catch William. He notices a tall blond. Pretty girl! Offers her a drink. She walks to a table as if she knows where she's going. Soft hair. Says her name is Carole. "You from around here?"

"Not really." She has a slow kind of voice.

So he guesses. "Not quite Southern."

She covers her eyes as if it's a game. "I'm thinking you're not local either." *Local.* This is the word William is always pushing her to say. He won't bother with this guy if he's from here.

The drinks arrive. Hers is a margarita. She sips at it.

"Want to dance?"

But she sees William giving her the signal. "Can you wait for me just a sec? My brother. He's keeping an eye on me."

Outside, William says, "What's the deal?" and a minute later, Hasker and William are sitting together at the table. Hasker talks about Red and William smiles. The music is loud. William is snapping his fingers and Maryann leans against Hasker. "So how long have you been out here?"

Hasker feels Maryann's nearness, smells the pleasantness of her hair.

William says, "We're going to a disco. Meet a guy about a music deal."

"You're in music. I figured. Like I've got friends in that world." Hasker asks what disco they're going to and says maybe he'll meet up with them later.

First there was the nice returned missionary and then there was this. He just moved in. He advanced on Maryann's heart and mind and house and they started to drink and have sex and he was always talking too fast; it all happened too fast. His hands and mouth were all over her. He was living in the place she kept so clean. He made her look at him. Listen to the music he liked. Drink beer. Iron a crease in his jeans. He was almost thirty. She'd been buried in her clean, stupid, sheltered life. He got fired for smoking in the back of the warehouse, but they were getting married; they were going someplace. They drank. They went to bed. He got a job pumping gas. He got fired again. In bed he was too fast, but it was understandable and they did it everyplace on the floor in bed in the car. They drank. They called her parents. He managed it. She was tired from getting up and he'd bother her. He'd call her at work. He'd say get me some money I'll meet you outside. He'd say get me some money I'm taking your car. He'd say get me some money I'm leaving you. Her parents should have locked her up. He'd tell her to cash a cheque and have money ready when he came by in her car. She couldn't concentrate. So she quit her job and got another one at a little restaurant in the mall, but he'd stand outside and watch and when he was watching she forgot who she was. It's hard to believe how she disappeared, but she'd known him a month and they were husband and wife. She had a duty and in Hawaii, when they got off the plane, didn't he know his way, didn't he know where he was? He called himself Spirit and she was supposed to carry his knife, which was like a seal, like something more meaningful than the wedding because he thought God did not exist and maybe He didn't but maybe He did and if she had him back the way he was when he slid up against her those first few days, she wouldn't care because he made her feel so sure when he did that, when he slid and pushed up against her. Sure of herself.

At 2:00 a.m. it's deserted out at Hanuama Bay. The moon is there behind clouds and the stars are reflected in dark, living water. A picture can be made of the sleeping fish, the coral reef, everything alive but asleep, and William tells Larry to get out of the car. There is the sound of water beating against land. Think of it. William was afraid she would go to the police. You could tease God and fool your parents and go home afterwards, but this was different. To know that you were living your life.

HONOLULU

47

I had thought of the end of this story as an afternoon on the old courthouse steps, Maryann's long blue muumuu starched by the trade winds as she stands looking out at the mountains, finally free. Mike Brennan is talking to the intern he's brought along from California. The two of them are tall and serious amid the various locals who mingle around the courthouse, many of whom are about to make their own pleas. Yes, Maryann is a dream we have dreamed, but instead of coming out of the old courthouse with victory dripping off of us like earned perspiration, we are going into a new circuit court building, wondering if we have identified each other accurately.

Mike Brennan looks assured, uncompromising, and as smart as I want him to be. Maryann has told me she feels good in his presence and I do too, although, when I speak to him in the hallway, when I slide in behind him as he steps into the courtroom, I have to pretend that I'm filling a necessary place, bearing witness because Maryann isn't here.

We've entered a panelled room without windows. There is the echo of thunder. The lawyers are saying, "This doesn't happen. I can't remember when . . ." and I think, Not since March of 1982. There was thunder then too.

Twenty-three years. Even without windows, I can feel the courtroom darken as the other team pulls out its heavy files. Someone named Fudo is going to represent Jan Futa and Colleen Hirai, who was dismissed as the first prosecutor in Maryann's trial. Could she have questioned the ethics of what the state was willing to do to win?

Doesn't matter. They'll put her away.

While Fudo and his assistant arrange papers on their table, another man comes in, tall, good-looking, salt-and-peppery Japanese. He has a familiar jutting chin and high cheekbones like a spoon with sharp edges. This must be Stephen Hioki, since he offers his help to Mike Brennan and then takes his leave.

Next, Judge Town enters and we are commanded to rise.

Brennan is trying to establish three things: first, that in 1982, the state failed to provide Maryann's defence with information about William's sentence in California; second, that it failed to disclose his jailhouse activities as a snitch; and third, that the state allowed William to perjure himself. Brennan says that Hioki was given an FBI rap sheet on William that was inaccurate. The reason this matters is that Hioki might have argued his case differently if he had known William's actual sentence. Judge Au might have made his decisions differently and the jury might have weighed William's testimony differently. If everyone had understood that William had the possibility of parole, they would have understood that he had something to gain by testifying against his wife.

On the stand, Colleen Hirai remembers nothing so Brennan gives up on her fairly quickly and calls Jan Futa, who prosecuted Maryann in 1982 and who has been fighting off this inquisition for five years. Even waiting to be called, she stood in the hall conferring with her lawyers, black shoe tapping at the polished floor. Wearing a good suit and shoulder-length hair, she is, like all of us, twenty-three years older. The spark is gone. In a surly voice she explains that she is a lawyer in private practice, and, yes, in 1982 she was a prosecutor. But it was a long time ago, she says, eerily echoing Maryann's words on the stand.

When Brennan asks if she remembers the trial, she stares at him. "It was a long time ago," she says again. As he

questions her, she insists that she does not remember anything. *There are many things she doesn't remember because it's
hard to fabricate things if there is no basis of truth.*

"If I showed you these documents, would they refresh
your memory?"

"Hmm." Leaning over. Frowning. "Well, I can't say
whether these are originals . . ." Futa has been given
several months to review the documents. The hearing has
been repeatedly delayed. What difference do any of us
make in the world? What matters? Two young people were
wicked and indifferent and cruel. They harmed and killed.
And there is no undoing such things; there is only to recognize and then to reclaim whatever can be saved.

Maryann's California case was heard by a Mormon
judge who was under investigation for making porno-
graphic phone calls and needed a conviction for his own
reasons. Her lawyer had never defended anyone before.
There was no jury in that trial and she was not called to
the stand. William was still telling her he would "take
the fall" and get her clear. He had taken that mysterious
bus ride to Yuma after she'd been arrested. He had gone
straight to her father. Following his instructions, she had
insisted that she was only driving Arauza's car because her
husband had given it to her. And the judge, who admitted
that there was no evidence that she had touched the gun
that killed Arauza, convicted her for being present when

Arauza was killed. The felony murder conviction was Maryann's, not William's. But that it was only the beginning of what the jury in Hawaii did not understand.

Now, Judge Town underlines the situation. "This is a big deal," he says, looking sternly at the lawyers. He adds that if the state is required to remedy the situation, it may decide to reduce Maryann's sentence.

But Brennan draws himself up and insists that they must overturn Maryann's conviction. Silence. I am the only spectator in the room. No reporter. No one from past or present. Judge Town is a small man with grey hair and a pink face. His voice is slightly falsetto.

Fudo, who has the face of a predator, says Hioki obviously knew William's sentence. He had to have known. Why not call him to refute or support . . . ?

The legal wrangling goes on all day. We had broken for lunch and I'd looked after Mike Brennan and his intern but gone my own way. I felt shy and covert. But in the courtroom, it was frustrating not to be able to interrupt. When Mike Brennan discussed the similar modus operandi between the California and Hawaii murders, he didn't mention the important similarity between the Leach and Hasker crimes. Same bar, same destination, same tricks. My father would have mentioned it, I was sure, to prove that Maryann was taking directions from William, as Joe Leach had said.

"Why bother the State of Hawaii with a proceeding that is trying to exonerate someone who was, at the very least, Your Honour, an accomplice to an extremely vicious murder?" Fudo had asked. But he did not use that argument more than once, which was interesting. The state, in 1982, had prosecuted Maryann as the shooter. It would not do to point out her role as partial accomplice now. It would look like the state had prosecuted and convicted the wrong person. "And why dredge up old bits and pieces of evidence that were fully examined to everyone's satisfaction twenty some years ago?" After all, Fudo implied, if nothing else Maryann went along with this loser. Too bad she's spending her sorry life in prison, but that's what happens when you pick someone up in a bar and leave him dead next to the highway.

Maybe. But doesn't it matter that she had a fair trial? Doesn't it matter that William perjured himself when he testified against her, that he was never charged with the murder, that he was the prime witness for the prosecution in spite of his history? Doesn't it matter that her lawyer never knew that William might have exchanged false testimony for an earlier parole? Doesn't truth, in its minutest particular, matter? Isn't that what we are after?

Or do we allow this conspiracy of silence?

I had reconnected with Maryann out of guilt, but there was more to it now and the next morning I was at the courthouse in time to buy a coffee in the shop just off the lobby. The coffee was in a pot on a hot plate and the woman who took my coins was blind, which seemed at that moment to be significant. Upstairs, I saw Stephen Hioki and when I introduced myself, he said, "On the jury? Still following the case?" Perhaps he has battled enough windmills. "I don't remember a whole lot about that trial," he said, "but I remember my moments with Maryann. I don't know what it was, but she was different than any other client I ever had."

Court was called into session. I was making notes in the old yellow notebook – the smooth yellow surface, the red spine. It was precisely when I realized that I would take it back to Hawaii, that I knew I had come this long journey with Maryann in order to finish the things left undone in my own life. There were blank pages at the back of the book. Bare lines. "The transcripts seem to indicate that I was under the impression," Hioki was saying, "that Mr. Acker had life without parole. It seems I was inter- ested in impeaching him because he couldn't have been convicted of felony murder if he was sentenced to life without parole. I was sure he was lying about the convic- tions because I had researched the law and that sentence would not have applied to that crime." I could see Hioki as a young man, ardent in his green pants and brown jacket. He thought William was the shooter in California, that he was lying about that on the stand because he would not have been sentenced to life without parole or otherwise. His questions had jumped around, he'd been given an inaccurate FBI rap sheet, but he had made one glaring mistake. I had read the old newspaper articles before I flew to Hawaii for this hearing and on March 24, 1982, a reporter for the *Star Bulletin*, Hawaii's evening paper, had reported that William Acker did, in fact, have the possibility of parole. Did the defence lawyer not read newspapers? Could he not have called California to check on William's sentence as that reporter must have done? An error of omission. An error of enormous consequence.

"I may have slowed down a little these days, Your Honour," Hioki noted, looking up at the judge, "but in those days I was relentless. I was passionate about holding the state to its burden of proof. I used up my fees before even coming to trial. There were only three witnesses to the murder and one was dead. I had to do everything in my power to show that Mr. Acker was not credible. I tried to prove his untruthfulness, to show that his version of the murder was false, that Mr. Hasker's shirt wasn't torn, that there were two bullets fired, not three. We had ballistics supporting our facts. Larry Hasker was shot from the back to the front at a fifteen-degree angle. But Mr. Acker said Maryann was facing him and fired three shots. I would have been glad to have a motive for his blaming

Maryann. To know that he had the possibility of parole, or to know that he was a jailhouse informant, would have helped my case!"

No wonder William had sat in the witness stand with a smirk on his face. He had not expected it to be so easy. Even now, his lethal spirit stalked the little courtroom so that the crossfire went on for two more hours until Fudo, who was in a hurry to pick up his daughter at school, said it boiled down to two different counsels having different strategies. Not so, Brennan said, making a final, stunning argument in Maryann's defence. "Two different strategies?" he sounded astounded. "The fact is," he said in a gravelly voice, "that there is no evidence in the record that says Hioki did *anything* for strategic reasons. This is not about Mr. Hioki's strategy. This is about the state's obligation. They were there to do justice, to get the right person convicted. And they failed to do that. They failed because they used the testimony of a witness who repeatedly perjured himself and who did so with their knowledge. They failed because they used the testimony of a witness who repeatedly sold himself to prosecutors. They had the obligation to tell defence that their prime witness was a known informant, and that he had turned state's evidence because he had been sentenced to life with the possibility of parole in California and was hoping to reduce his ultimate sentence."

Judge Town had worked with Fudo and Hioki and Jan Futa many times over the years. As he put it, "I've had each of you in my courtroom; we know each other well." It was not pleasant to contemplate wrongdoing on the part of any of these colleagues. There were reputations at stake, including his own.

48

I spent a day retracing Maryann's steps. It was going to be several months before Judge Town made his decision. But there I was, back in the realm of the past, so I went to the street where Maryann and William had briefly lived. The Makiki Arms is gone now, but there are still similar two-storey buildings nearby. I spent a summer in one of them when I visited my brother and his first wife in 1958. Their baby, my nephew, was six months old, and I used to push him around the neighbourhood in his stroller, feeling pleased with my newfound grown-up self. Now there are broken-down cars in the driveway and a tall building taking up most of the yard where I used to hang the diapers when we did the wash. Thurston is on a rise and I used to look down at the harbour, with its ships and the

Aloha Tower. How, I wondered, would Maryann ever adapt to so much change?

The second-floor balcony of the Makiki Arms had run across the front of the building. Underneath, on ground level, were the laundry room and the pay phone and the washing machine where William hid the gun. In front was the parking lot, where he put Larry Hasker's car when he took him upstairs. A little later – not much later – William and Larry and Maryann came back down. Larry's hands were tied behind his back and his shirt was riding his shoulders. Larry was saying, "Ah come on, man, are you serious?"

William told Larry that he was.

From Thurston and the non-existent Makiki Arms, I drove to the building where Larry Hasker once lived with his sister, Kimberly. It still looms in an ugly way over the main commercial corner near the university, and I had a beer in Puck's Alley, where I used to go on long, warm afternoons. I thought, Is this Maryann's past or mine?

Before I left Hawaii in 1982, I drove completely around the island to say goodbye. It was like drowning – passing the house I used to visit in spite of a kitchen full of rats, the garbage, and the stories of a child punished in the closet. How to explain the wretched pleasure of that nasty bedroom with its tilted bureau mirror, the attraction I had once felt for the man who lived in that filthy place? Then down the road to my best friend's house, where she lived all alone, where she was raped, where her dog was killed, where the screen porch is something she built by and for herself. Just a shack, now that I look at it, but a room of her own. And farther on to the place where both my parents sat one day, Mother saying, "Let's have our lunch here." My father had parked the car and we had pretended happiness. It was the last time I would see him alive.

Up by Haleiwa, the preschool I visited when I worked in child care. The lukewarm welcome and the hot lunch. I had an office on the second floor of a Congregational church on the outskirts of Kailua. It was an agency that provided federally funded child care to low-income families, some of them local and some remnants of families like mine who had left the mainland during the 1960s. The white women were single mothers like me, divorced, living far from home. The local families were poor but intact.

My office window overlooked a marsh that had once been part of the sea and on its edge sat the remains of an ancient *heiau* called Ulupo – a great level platform of stones, very potent, very carefully placed. At night I went back to my children and stared into the darkness of the garden, trying to understand the mysteries of the island, the bloodlines, the descent from gods to mortals, the antagonism against people who come from outside.

Someday, I told myself, I'll come back to Hawaii and drive along any street, any beach road and know that I made a difference to this place. I'll be able to say, here's X's house or Y's. The Buddhist Temple Michael and I visited that day we knew everything. The cove where we swam. And the house of the former prosecutor. The one who said, They'll put her away.

Instead, it was another trail entirely that I was following. Instead, I drove to the Hilton, where William and Maryann met Larry Hasker and Joe Leach. The Garden Bar is gone like so much else, but I went out and watched three or four children scraping around in the sand that covered the spot where Maryann had danced with Joe after she ordered her drink.

Then I had a great desire to see my old house, to see what had become of it and how I would feel standing in the shade of the front-yard tree. It was a fig, with big stiff leaves. "Ours was a 3 bedroom, 2 bath house, no garage, but a covered carport," Maryann had finally written, trying to describe her childhood home. "The kitchen, narrow and long, was at the front, with a window facing the street above the sink." I had waited five years for that description, but everything that matters was left out – whatever it was that happened within those walls, and the child, and the reason her need to be needed was so great.

In truth, the fig tree is gone and it was hard to imagine us there: my girls with long hair and long legs running up the street as if everything – the dolls and stuffed animals, the dog, the friends, and the grandmother – would not disappear.

On the way to Kailua, I had gone the long way out of Waikiki. The day was beautifully clear, with the hills shouting their greens on the left side of the highway and the ocean swirling on the right. There is the expensive suburb of Black Point and then Kahala and after that I could smell the old, dry dustiness of the soil as I drove beyond houses and gardens and along the barren expanse of rocky beach that stretches to Koko Head, that startling crater that rises up on one side of Hanauma Bay. There is a legend that involves a beautiful girl who is fought over by two young men. Fearing the rivals will harm themselves, she turns herself into this crater, sacrificing her life. Her father stretches out to protect her, forming the arms of Hanauma Bay. There was Larry and William. And Maryann. Bert Bray reaching out to his child but unwilling to sell his house for her. There was another family as well, another child. The night before I'd dreamed about my mother sitting at the table I was trying to set. I was trying to do my best, but her best dishes, the family heirlooms, kept shattering in my hands.

I drove past Koko Head. In the distance, as I curled in and out of the curves in the road, I caught glimpses of the windward side – Makapu, Lanikai, and the twin islands we once knew like friends. Then I pulled off the road, preparing myself for the sadness I'd feel at the murder site. How eerie and fugitive I felt, as if I should mark the spot with one of those Mexican crosses, or leave a sacred stone wrapped in a fresh ti leaf.

I got out of the car as Larry and Joe had done and looked down at the bay.

It is different now. There are hundreds of people on the sand. There is a building. There is a ticket booth. There is an educational video and an entrance fee.

Hard to imagine a murder. In such a place.

Except that up near the highway, there is still the rutted road and those brambly kiawe trees. There is still a drop that hasn't been smoothed and the spirits that stick to this place, and I could imagine Maryann and her brand-new husband spending the night in one of the hillside caves. In the morning, waking up, feeling the sunrise slippery and fast, did they swim? Did they spend the next hours with the tourists looking at fish or did they climb back up to the highway and wait for the bus to take them back to a day of planning and arguing. In her letters and conversations, Maryann never says what they did. What she says is, if you like who you are now, you have to accept your past.

At the hearing, when Mike Brennan described the murder of Cesario Arauza to Judge Town, he said it was done "execution-style." He said Arauza's arms were crossed over his chest, he was lying on his back, and he had been shot in the head. "Do you think an eighteen-year-old girl is physically capable of that?" The conversation took place during a recess and I was listening, sitting on the sidelines with my notebook, more or less out of sight. Hearing Brennan's words, I felt real surprise. He wasn't working to overturn Maryann's conviction because it was theoretically possible or because he had students who needed the work. Mike Brennan believed in her innocence.

There was dismay too, which was another surprise. Because if Maryann isn't guilty, my own guilt is worse.

Those lost five minutes that cost her life.

Leaving Honolulu, we took off to windward, as usual, flying over Pearl Harbor and the Aloha Tower and then I could see the palace, white in the sunlight, as if that little monarchy ever stood a chance. I've watched the coastline of O'ahu diminish so many times, ever farther and farther away, that from above it looks like the back of my hand, as familiar to me as fingers, knuckles, veins, and wrist. There is the sky and the light and the swallowing sea and the beautiful circular bay and who, in such a severe and archaic place, could kidnap and rob and kill?

Squinting, I could almost see the events taking place. 1978. The risen moon. The tiny tableau. In an old album, there is a picture of two little girls standing at its cusp looking down at the ocean where the water curls in and out over the reef and where, at night, there is that absent planet, fallen like Lucifer, lit by the moon. Now, looking down at the surf, where children are still and forever playing, I thought of the moray eel I met in that same reef long ago. My brother must have been somewhere ahead, not far away, urging me on, but he was not near enough to save me from the sight of the open mouth and throat. Years of remembering and still there is no way of knowing how such a creature does what he does or sees what he sees of the world.

In January, three months after the trial, Judge Town overturned Maryann's 1982 conviction. Local papers again painted her as the villain. TWO-TIME KILLER GRANTED A NEW TRIAL, read a headline in the *Advertiser*. "He did it! He did it!" I shouted into the phone, because Maryann could not get through to Mike Brennan. I could hear her initial scream of excitement. I could hear her shouting to her friends and to Jesse the dog. Then Maryann got quiet. "I'll be here a while yet," she said. "The state will appeal. Mike will offer them a deal and they won't take it. So there will have to be another trial. It could take years."

49

This year we have goldfinches flashing through the birch tree, where the leaves, turning autumn yellow, make them impossible to see. One hundred years ago, Ayn Rand was born. There is a wolf in a nearby field. Valere has been released. There are photographs of her standing on a California beach.

This year, I walk to the bank of the river, moving down the rocks like an animal because I know this patch of earth in my muscles by now. The ground between the house and the river is covered by pine needles, so it's slippery and I move under the enormous trees, which are black as silhouettes.

In late August the water is a shock. Three minutes, Michael promises. When I plunge then, it is for his smile.

Today I notice the wavering lines of light on the trunk of a tree, alternating ribbons of dark and light. Michael is several yards ahead of me, but I shout, "What makes it do that?" I see, now, that trees all around me are doing this – reflecting light. Their trunks and branches appear to be decomposing and I'm astonished and dismayed that every morning I've stayed in bed drinking coffee while all this has been going on.

Across from us are the rapids, which pour and pour until they freeze in the winter and then break up and pour again. Around us, in a great circle, are the riverbanks, except where the channel of the smaller branch of the river cuts in quietly, shallow and swampy, with its beautiful bridge. No more burning, I promise myself, and I swim in the other direction, west, across to the rapids where it's possible to climb out and lie on the rocks where we often make picnics, taking the food across by canoe: tomatoes, fresh bread, onions, cheese, beer, and fruit. Farther up, we poured in the ashes of my brother and his wife after they died in the crash. But Michael and I are two heads now, moving along like water rats on the surface of this black water, the house back in the trees, where it looks like some-thing we have allowed to happen, containing only toler-ance and a hundred after-dinner dances when the table has been pushed aside. Here, while Maryann has been living her life in prison, we have been collecting meals, group and solo swims, games of badminton, flowers and vegetables, children and friends, dogs and jokes, hearts and charades, joy and grief.

ACKNOWLEDGEMENTS

My father taught me to think and my mother taught me to tell. I rejoice in these talents and am forever grateful to my parents. I am grateful to Sarah Collins, in Honolulu, who kept me in touch with the legal manoeuvrings there and helped me find people who were lost along with records and articles in various archives. I thank my initial readers: Barbara Gowdy, Constance Rooke, Esta Spalding, Kristin Sanders, and Michael Ondaatje. A reader is the best help a writer can have. Each of these infused the story with insight, ideas, and perspective. I thank Michael Brennan and Dan Weiss and the others who have represented Maryann in her legal efforts over many years. I thank them for that and for being helpful to me. I thank David Fyfe for research, Bill and Sakurako Fisher for particular kindness during the writing of this book, and Susie

Schlesinger for being there. I thank Susan Renouf, at McClelland & Stewart, who did more than edit this book, who acted as its shepherd and guardian from the first moment it was suggested to her. No book without Susan. Certainly not the same book. Then, I thank Ellen Levine, my more than agent, who cares about content and meaning and getting it right. I thank Heather Sangster for final touches. I thank Michael, again, as my partner in life and the one who encouraged me and listened to me think and helped me seek out the bone truth of my connection to Maryann Acker, who is the most important person of all to thank. Thank you, Maryann.